The Stem Cell Debate

FACETS

Select Titles in the Facets Series

The Stem Cell Debate

Ted Peters

Fortress Press
Minneapolis

Cover image: Cell injection, copyright © Image Source/
Corbis. Used by permission.
Cover design: Jessica Puckett

Scripture quotations are from the New Revised Standard
Version Bible, copyright © 1989 by the Division of Christian
Education of the National Council of the Churches of Christ
in the USA. Used by permission. All rights reserved.

Library of Congress Cataloging-in-Publication Data

Library of Congress Publication Data available.

ISBN: 978-0-8006-6229-5

The paper used in this publication meets the minimum
requirements of American National Standard for Information Sciences–Permanence of Paper for Printed Library
Materials, ANSI Z329.48-1984.

Manufactured in the U.S.A.
11   10   09   08   07   1   2   3   4   5   6   7   8   9   10

Contents

Preface

The global controversy over stem cell research is like a baseball diamond. Beginning with science at home plate, no one scores until they have touched the three bases: religion, ethics, and politics.

The good news for persons of religious faith is that they can go to bat in the public policy debates over what direction science should be going. Religious voices are being listened to, even if argued against. This is a time in which our church leaders are being called to engage in serious theological reflection regarding what we believe constitutes human nature and human destiny; and they are being called to formulate ethical counsel that will be taken seriously by the society that surrounds us. This is a time for theologians to be on their good behavior.

Just what is at stake? A superficial reading of news reports might lead one to surmise that the central issue is one of protecting innocent human embryos from destruction at the hand of baby-killing scientists. We are told again and again that the battle against stem cells is another front in the battle against elective abortion. The passion and energy that had been marshaled in fighting over abortion have been re-deployed to the stem cell debate. The integrity of many Christians is judged by whether they courageously sign up to fight on the right side, the side of protecting innocent embryos from laboratory execution in the name of big science.

In this little book, I will ask the reader to be patient, to take the time to penetrate below such superficial treatments. Under the layer of rhetorical steam lies a fascinating realm of wondrous science, theological inquiry, ethical deliberation, and public policy. The scientific achievements to date are astounding in their complexity; and, even more importantly, they promise perhaps the biggest revolution in medical therapy yet achieved in the modern world. The scientific discoveries regarding the role of genes in human biology prod theologians to return to their anthropological drawing boards, to review again just how we should understand the human person in light of our divine creation and our divine destiny. Once this fundamental theological work has been done, then religiously committed ethicists would be ready to draw on solid intellectual resources in both science and faith to render moral counsel that could guide our society wisely through a period of increased choice and opportunity. Public leaders who are responsive to religious voices within their

constituency need to study theological understandings of human nature as they seek to regulate
scientific research. A healthy public conversation
could circle and re-circle the bases from science
back to science, touching religion and ethics and
politics on the way.

Like a doctor, I would like to provide a diagnosis and a prescription. Most of what follows in
this Facets book will be diagnosis. I will attempt
to describe what is going on. I will attempt to
provide an analysis of the worldwide stem cell
controversy that will show that this is not merely
another skirmish in the abortion battle. What is in
fact going on is delightfully complex and exceed-
ingly important, but important in ways that those
whose eyes are fixed on the abortion debate are
simply blind to.

Here is the symptom requiring diagnosis. The
public policy debates are primarily debates over
the ethics of human embryonic stem cell research.
Yet these debates seem to go nowhere. Adversaries
talk past one another, rather than engaging one
another's issues head on.

Why? Here is the diagnosis. What enters the
public debate as moral arguments come from at
least three different ethical frameworks. A framework is not a moral argument in itself. Rather, it is
a set of assumptions regarding human nature and
our ethical responsibility. Regardless of whether
we side with or against stem cell research, these
assumptions frame our moral argument. The
three frameworks operative in the current debate

over stem cells can be identified as these: (1) the embryo protection framework, (2) the nature protection framework, and (3) the medical benefits framework.

Within each of the three ethical frameworks one might argue either in opposition to stem cell research or in favor of research. What distinguishes each framework is its own focal question. Within the embryo protection frame the central question is: is human embryonic stem cell research a form of abortion; and, if so, are laboratory scientists baby-killers? Within the nature protection frame the central question is: are scientists manipulating the genetic nature of human beings to such an extent that they "play God" and risk hurling our society down a path toward a *Brave New World*? Within the medical benefits frame the central question is: could regenerative medicine provide a leap forward in the relief of human suffering and the enhancement of human flowering; and, if so, is the opportunity itself a sufficient moral warrant for supporting it? The moral arguments pro and con that rise up out of each of these three are distinct. We cannot explain why we are talking past one another unless we understand the distinct frameworks.

That is my diagnosis. Now, I will add a prescription. My prescription is that our society should support human embryonic stem cell research and the development of regenerative medicine. We should encourage our best scientists to do their best work; and we should encourage them to work with as much alacrity as possible. I recommend this for theological reasons. My theologically grounded ethical arguments begin from within the medical benefits framework; but I feel obligated to support my position by arguing as well from within the embryo protection and nature protection frameworks.

The distinction between diagnosis and prescription ought to be clear. You the reader may not like my prescription. Even so, this should not discourage you from benefiting from the present book. The diagnosis can still be quite helpful, even if you elect a different therapy.

Before proceeding into the book's content directly, I would like to pause and offer some background information. I am not a scientist. Nor am I a politician. Rather, I am a theologian for whom theology entails ethics; and I have been functioning as a bioethicist now for a decade and a half.

My focus of research and study has been the interaction of faith and culture. Because natural science plays such an influential role not only in Western Enlightenment culture but now in globalization, I have given much of the last two decades to the dialogue between Christian theology and research science.

Beginning in 1990, I served as Principal Investigator on what was said by James Watson to be the first grant ever given by the U.S. National Institutes of Health to a theologian. Federal money permitted me and my colleagues at the Center for Theology and the Natural Sciences in Berkeley to study the

"Theological and Ethical Questions Raised by the Human Genome Project." I put together a team of molecular biologists, behavioral geneticists, philosophers, theologians, and ethicists. We monitored the Human Genome Project for its first four years. This provided me with an opportunity to gain a lay person's sophistication in basic genetics as well as watch the fast-moving frontier of laboratory research.

Immediately on the heels of this study, I was invited by the American Association for the Advancement of Science in Washington, D.C., to work with a team of scientists and ethicists on issues surrounding intellectual property. Specifically, we confronted the question of patenting raw genomic information that was emerging from the Human Genome Project. I took the side of those who think we should go slowly. That is, we should refrain from filing for patents on raw genomic data. Patents should be granted only on downstream genetic products that would have utility for medical therapy.

Then, beginning in 1996, I unknowingly became involved in what would become the worldwide controversy over human embryonic stem cells. I along with my colleagues at the Graduate Theological Union were asked to serve as consultants in the work of Michael D. West, then CEO of the Geron Corporation. West has since moved to Advanced Cell Technology (ACT) in Boston. Significant here is the fact that it was Geron who funded the research that led to James

Thomson's historic isolation and characterization of human pluripotent stem cells in August 1998. By that time I had signed on as a member of the Ethics Advisory Committee (EAB) at Geron. For four years in virtual secrecy I could watch the fast-moving frontier of laboratory research and take measure of the volcano that could soon erupt in both scientific breakthroughs and ethical sparks.

More recently, the voters of California, the state where I live, passed Proposition 71 in 2004. This established the California Institute for Regenerative Medicine (CIRM). Having approved $3 billion in bonds to support stem cell research, we expect the next chapter in genetic history to be written in this west coast state. As I write this, I serve on the Scientific and Medical Accountability Standards Working Group for CIRM, which sets ethical standards and regulates research.

I recite this brief history to demonstrate that this systematic theologian with an interest in ethics has had the opportunity to follow the rapidly moving frontier of primary genetic research for nearly two decades. I find myself with both the opportunity and perhaps the responsibility to ask what implications new genetic knowledge might have for the Christian understanding of human nature, as well as to ask just what moral counsel I could offer a society confronted with so many new and unprecedented choices.

The insights I share with you in what follows are not the product of individual experience or genius. I have been blessed by bright and charitable colleagues who have provided me with indispensable dialogue partners. In particular, I must make mention of two very special colleagues, who are also my friends. The first is Karen Lebacqz, who has taught Christian Ethics at Pacific School of Religion and the Graduate Theological Union (GTU) for nearly three decades. Karen was the first chair of the Geron EAB. Her stress on the justice concerns for access by the poor to future stem cell therapies will be reflected in the pages that follow. The second is Gaymon Bennett, who is finishing up his doctoral studies in systematic theology at the GTU. Gaymon served as EAB research assistant during the period that Geron was experimenting with its initial four cell lines. It is Gaymon's analysis of the present situation that has led to the diagnosis: public policy debates operate from within three distinct ethical frameworks. Much of the background research for this book was derived in concert with Karen and Gaymon, and I'm grateful for their permission to incorporate here the results of some of our shared labors.

As we proceed, we will briefly review the science of stem cells and regenerative medicine. Then we will turn to the three ethical frameworks within which moral reasoning takes place. Following this, we will look at a fourth framework, the secular framework within which ethical guidelines and even regulations are currently being formulated to guide scientific work. As we analyze these various ethical frameworks, we will engage in theological reflection regarding human nature. On this basis, we will offer reasons why a person of Christian faith can, in good conscience, find justification for encouraging the advance of science toward the end of relieving human suffering and promoting human flourishing. Finally, we will ask whether a theologically informed ethicist can help guide us through this period of civilization when we are inundated with unavoidable yet important choices.

1.

The Science of Stem Cells

In recent stem cell debates, the focus of science and ethics is on pluripotent human embryonic stem cells (hES cells). Are there other kinds of stem cells? Oh, yes. We will describe the family of stem cells and all their relatives in the paragraphs ahead. But first we look at the theory of regenerative medicine and the role that stem cells might play in developing new therapies.

As one might surmise from the term *regenerative*, the goal here is to develop a form of medical therapy that regenerates damaged or deteriorating tissue. When a person is a victim of a heart attack, for example, the heart muscle is damaged. Quick medical attention can arrest the deterioration that is threatening. But, to date, no way has been devised for regenerating the heart muscle itself. Whatever loss occurs is permanent. The patient lives on with increased risk that the next incident could be fatal.

What if we could insert into the damaged heart tissue a colony of cells that would regenerate the damaged tissue? This is exactly the promise of pluripotent embryonic stem cells. Stem cells create new tissue. They could renew that broken heart. In fact, early experiments suggest that transplanted hES cells could actually restore the damaged heart to a level of health and function that surpasses the one that suffered in the first place. Regenerative medicine promises to go beyond stopping deterioration to provide the power of organ renewal. Although it is by no means a sure thing, we could be finding ourselves on the eve of a magnificent revolution in medical science.

What scientists are imagining is placing regenerative stem cells into not only the heart but also the brain, pancreas, liver, and spinal nervous system. With tissue renewal, regenerative therapy could reverse deterioration that leads to such diseases as heart disease, Alzheimer's, Parkinson's, diabetes, lower body paralysis, and numerous others. As a by-product, regenerative medicine offers strides forward in the battle against cancer. Excitement has been rising for nearly a decade now. Hope is high. The challenge might be more difficult than putting earthlings on the moon a half-century ago; but many scientists are rising up to meet this complex yet promising challenge.

What kind of stem cells are we talking about?

A stem cell is a cell that makes more cells. It is a progenitor cell from which tissues stem. "Stem cells are defined functionally as cells that have the capacity to self-renew as well as the ability to generate differentiated cells. More specifically, stem cells can generate daughter cells identical to their mother (self-renewal) as well as produce progeny with more restricted potential (differentiated cells)."[1]

We can rank stem cells according to potency. On the top of the list we find the *totipotent stem cell.* As the name implies, it is totally potent. It can duplicate itself by making more totipotent cells. And, if located in a mother's body, it can make a baby.

On the next step down the list we find the pluripotent stem cell. Like the totipotent cell, the pluripotent cell can replicate itself. These cells are self-renewing. In fact, under the right conditions where they receive appropriate nourishment, pluripotent cells can divide and replicate themselves indefinitely. Scientists early on said a line of pluripotent stem cells would be considered "immortal," because they could replace themselves without deterioration forever. Rather than use the theological word "immortal," today scientists refer to a self-renewing line of pluripotent cells as "characterized."

What distinguishes a characterized pluripotent stem cell is its capacity to make any and every tissue in the body. We say it is "undifferentiated," meaning that it has not yet committed itself to becoming a single tissue or even the progenitor of a single tissue. Rather, it is the progenitor from which all tissues in the body stem. It cannot make a baby. But it can make everything else.

What is so valuable to medical researchers is that pluripotent stem cells have the capacity of integrating into a tissue and becoming a stem cell for that tissue. Already pluripotent stem cells have been teased into becoming cardiomyocytes, pulsating heart tissue. In principle, if we place pluripotent stem cells into bone marrow, they will provide new blood cells that could be used to combat leukemia. If we place pluripotent stem cells in the brain, they will become the host tissue, creating new and healthy nerve cells, overcoming the damage done by Parkinson's and Alzheimer's diseases. Pluripotent stem cells can be made into pancreatic islet cells used to combat diabetes.

What is key here is that pluripotent stem cells have the plasticity to integrate with the host tissue. As we continue down the hierarchy of stem cells, they become increasingly differentiated and, therefore, tissue-specific. They lose their plasticity.

A *multipotent stem cell*, for example, retains some but not all of the plasticity of the pluripotent cell. It is capable of making new cells within the range of a specific tissue type, whether it be endoderm, mesoderm, or ectoderm. Hematopoietic or blood stem cells within the mesoderm tissue type, for example, can make two different kinds of blood cells, red and white. But multipotent hematopoietic stem cells cannot make brain cells. Experiments have demonstrated this.

A *unipotent stem cell,* as the name indicates, is capable of creating only one kind of tissue. Although unipotent cells have some capacity for renewal, they are sufficiently differentiated that their plasticity has disappeared.

Some cells still with multipotency seem to stick around in one's body for the span of the person's life. These have been called *adult stem cells* and have been found in the blood stream and nervous system. They are already partially differentiated; yet they have the capacity to replicate themselves as well as create new cells in the blood system, nervous system, and elsewhere. "Adult stem cells are generated during development beyond the stage of gastrulation" where they become "mesoderm, endoderm, and ectoderm: subsequently, tissue-specific fate decisions are made. Therefore, adult stem cells have lost pluripotency."[2] Adult stem cells do not have the all-important ability pluripotent stem cells have, namely, the plasticity to integrate and become any and every tissue.

(See figure on next page.)

Where do we get pluripotent human embryonic stem cells?

Before examining what happens in the laboratory with stem cells, let's remind ourselves of what embryogenesis looks like within a woman's body. Prior to fertilization, the woman contributes an egg and the man contributes a sperm. Egg and sperm are called *gametes.* During fertilization, the

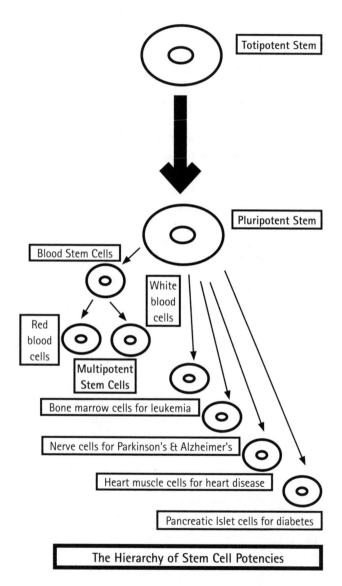

The Hierarchy of Stem Cell Potencies

egg absorbs the sperm. Some have tried to spread an image that the sperm drives itself into the egg, penetrating it. This is an analogy to what happens when human beings are having sexual intercourse. What actually happens at the biological level does not imitate what happens at the social level, however. Multiple sperm rest in the fur of the much larger egg's surface. The egg absorbs one sperm, allowing it to enter. As it is about to enter, the egg expels half of its chromosomes. The original 46 chromosomes are now reduced to 23. The sperm provides another 23. So, as soon as the sperm enters, the egg shuts the door to any additional sperm and rests with a full complement of 46 chromosomes. This fertilized egg is called a *zygote*, indicating that two things have combined into one.

In the days following, the zygote divides. It replicates itself. It divides into two cells. Then four. Then eight. At each of these divisions, every cell, now called a *blastomere*, is totipotent. It is capable of making an entire human being. If the cells remain tight together, only one baby will result. If the cells become separated into two, then it could lead to monozygotic or identical twins. Identical twins come from a single zygote. Similarly, if disaggregation occurs when four blastomeres are present, then quadruplets might be the result. Identical triplets usually indicate that early on there had been four, but only three came to term.

In the case of prize bulls out on the farm, livestock breeders commonly take the early embryo at the eight-cell stage and disaggregate it. Then they place each of the blastomeres into eight different cows. The result is the birth of eight bulls, all with the same genetic code. To date, it is uncommon practice for a woman's ob-gyn to recommend this method for human family planning.

Embryogenesis continues into the *blastocyst* stage. Between days four and six, an external shell of sorts grows to surround the inner cell mass. Called the *trophectoderm*, this surrounding tissue will eventually provide the connection with the uterine wall of the mother. What lies within the blastocyst is a collection of forty to a hundred cells. No longer possessing the totipotency of the earlier blastomeres, these have become the pluripotent progenitor cells.

If the mother's body does not flush the early embryo, then it will begin the process of gastrulation, when the inner cells begin to commit themselves to one of three families of tissue: endoderm, mesoderm, or ectoderm. What were previously pluripotent cells become multipotent cells. Then, between day 12 and 14, something of potential ethical importance happens. Now umbilically connected to the mother's body, the embryo develops a primitive streak, a line that indicates where the backbone will eventually appear. This stage is important for two reasons. First, once the primitive streak has appeared, we now have an individual for the first time. Up until this moment, the embryonic material could divide into twins. Or two units of embryonic material could combine to form a single one. With the appearance of the primitive streak, nature now knows how many babies-to-be the mother is pregnant with.

Another item is worth noting. Once the interaction between mother and embryo is established, the mother's hormones communicate with the genes of the lodger in her womb. Even though the embryo relies upon its full complement of genes on its 46 chromosomes, it is the mother's hormones which govern which genes turn on and that fetal development takes place. Without this relationship, embryonic material could not develop toward becoming a human person.

Now, let us take a look at what happens in the laboratory, *ex vivo*. Where does the scientist begin? The scientist needs to start with a zygote, or its equivalent. Where might one find a zygote? One place is in an IVF (*in vitro* fertilization) clinic. When a couple goes to such a clinic, eggs are removed from the mother and sperm from the father and combined in a petri dish. Perhaps a half dozen or a dozen fertilizations take place. If two or three are implanted in the mother, the remainder are frozen for storage. If the pregnancy takes and a child is born, the unimplanted or spare embryos sit in the freezer. This provides one source researchers can go to for embryonic material.

After thawing out the frozen material, the zygote is activated. Then it starts down the path toward blastocyst development. When it arrives at the blastocyst stage, the trophechtoderm is removed and the inner cell mass is disaggregated.

The individual cells are placed on a feeder tray. If the scientists do things right and if they are very lucky, the colony of pluripotent cells will divide naturally and, after fifty cell divisions without any deterioration, they will be defined as "characterized." This ability to self-renew while maintaining full pluripotency leads to descriptors such as "unlimited" or "continuous" or "capable of extensive proliferation."[3] Once characterized, experiments to tease pluripotent cells into integrating with targeted tissue can begin.

So the source for pluripotent hES cells is the blastocyst, about four to six days after zygote activation. Researchers to date have utilized blastocysts that are *ex vivo*, in a laboratory petri dish, *in vitro*. Scientists have not drawn them from a mother's body, *in vivo*, even though procedures such as this are now being proposed.[4]

Ex vivo, in the laboratory, these first few days of embryogenesis mimic what would be taking place within a mother's body. As the *ex vivo* embryo passes through gastrulation and approaches day 12 or 14, its development cannot rely upon hormonal signaling from the mother. Individuation does not take place. Normal fetal development is rendered impossible. Without an unforeseeable and unimaginable invention in artificial incubation, no child will ever be born outside a mother's womb.

Are spare embryos obtained from IVF clinics the only source? Not necessarily. In principle, scientists could actually perform the equivalent of *in vitro* fertilization in the laboratory and create their own zygote. Of the original four characterized hES cell lines created by James Thomson at the University of Wisconsin, three were drawn from frozen embryos and one was fresh. What has not yet been determined is whether the quality of thawed frozen embryos is satisfactory, or whether fresh embryos would be preferable. To date, first-level quality frozen embryos seem to be satisfactory.

(See figure on next page.)

Will cloning appear on the research horizon?

As we look toward the future, we can forecast that nuclear transfer, otherwise known as cloning, might be used to create a zygote. Why?

Here is the problem that needs solving. Suppose researchers would be successful at creating a colony of pluripotent hES cells that are ready for implantation in a patient's heart. The aim of such therapy would be to regenerate a particular person's heart tissue. However, just any ol' stem cells will not do. Any attempt to insert stem cells into a person's heart would arouse the immune defense system. The immune system would treat the stem cells as invading foreigners. It would reject the introduced stem cells and prevent their integration into the host heart tissue.

Given this prospect of immunal rejection, scientists have asked if cloning might come to the rescue. If the stem cells in question could be cloned

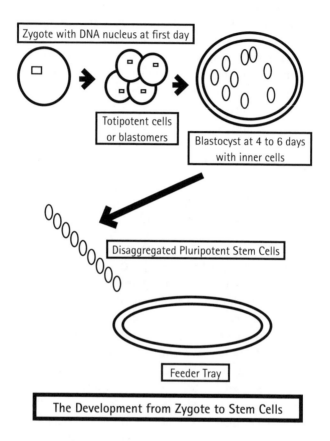

Zygote with DNA nucleus at first day

Totipotent cells
or blastomers

Blastocyst at 4 to 6 days
with inner cells

Disaggregated Pluripotent Stem Cells

Feeder Tray

The Development from Zygote to Stem Cells

from the patient, then they would be welcomed into the heart as if they belonged there. No immunal rejection would take place. Could we make pluripotent hES cells that would be patient-specific by creating zygotes with the patient's own genetic code? This leads us to the prospect of DNA nuclear transfer, commonly known as cloning.

In the case of DNA nuclear transfer, scientists would begin with a woman's egg. They would remove the entire DNA nucleus, not just 23 but all 46 chromosomes. The ennucleated egg would be called an *oocyte.* Lab technicians would not fertilize this oocyte. Rather, they would select a smaller differentiated cell—perhaps a skin cell—belonging to a future patient. They would try to dedifferentiate it—that is, they would try to run it back to its predifferentiated state. Then, scientists would place this dedifferentiated DNA nucleus in the oocyte. Once activated, this zygote would enter embryogenesis with the previously selected genetic code. If this genetic code matches that of the future patient, the result would be patient-specific pluripotent hES cells.

This method is technically called *somatic cell nuclear transfer* (SCNT) or *nuclear transfer* (NT) for short. What we are talking about here is the method of cloning developed by Ian Wilmut at Roslin Institute in Scotland. By this method Wilmut brought the sheep Dolly into the world. However, when it comes to stem cell research, no reproductive cloning would take place. Cloning in the form of nuclear transfer would be pressed into the service of providing patient specific pluripotent stem cells.

How far has the science come?

It was August 1998 when the first pluripotent human embryonic stem cells were isolated and characterized. Previously, in 1994, a Singapore researcher, Ariff Bongso, had isolated hES cells.[5] But it was not until 1998 that such isolated cells could also be characterized. This was accomplished by James Thomson at the University of Wisconsin, who established the first four lines which, as of this writing, joyously continue to proliferate.[6] Thomson was working on a contract with funding supplied by Michael D. West, then CEO of the Geron Corporation. Thomson needed private funding, because government restrictions against destroying embryos in research prevented federal funding.

Immediately, loyal Wisconsin Badgers quizzed themselves: could there be a cash cow here? Yes, was the forecast. With alacrity, the Wisconsin Alumni Research Foundation (WARF) filed for patents on Thomson's discoveries. Because the University of Wisconsin is a state-supported institution, it ought not to become a for-profit business. WARF is a for-profit business, created to zip all profits to the University of Wisconsin. WARF filed for and obtained two decisively important patents with the U.S. Patent and Trademark Office.[7] Just how much cash the cow will kick out only the future will tell.

The Geron Corporation obtained an exclusive license to research six cell types that might be grown from the WARF cell lines: liver, muscle, nerve, pancreas, blood, and bone. Geron is currently working on therapies for cardiac, nervous system, and pancreatic cells.

Although the spotlight was on the University of Wisconsin, in the dark something else potentially important was happening at Johns Hopkins University. John Gearhart announced in September 1998 that he had isolated human germ cells, hEG cells.[8] Also working with Geron funding, Gearhart derived his cells not from activated zygotes but rather from aborted fetuses at the five- to eight-week stage of development. The primordial germ ridge of such fetuses contains cells with the full complement of 46 chromosomes that are as yet undifferentiated. Could we make pluripotent stem cells from these? What Gearhart accomplished was their isolation. What has not yet been accomplished and remains on the research agenda is characterizing hEG cells and getting them to cooperate when trying to integrate them into host tissue.

All of this research was conducted with funds other than those supplied by the U.S. National Institutes of Health. On August 9, 2001, President George W. Bush went on television to announce a policy decision to maintain a government ban on funding any research that would involve the destruction of embryos. Yet he offered an exception. Research that employed the already existing characterized pluripotent stem cell lines could receive federal funding. The president mistakenly thought there might be 60 or even 72 such lines in existence. Scientists in the know could identify only one to two dozen such lines that had been fully characterized and would be fully ready for this research.

With the door to U.S. federal funds now definitively shut for the foreseeable future, scientific researchers continued their migration toward private funding and toward governments other than Uncle Sam. The government of Singapore established Biopolis, a seven-building research center, which has become a dream laboratory with all the most up-to-date equipment in order to seduce the world's scientists to come to Asia. The state of California passed Proposition 71 in 2004, voting three billion dollars in bond money to support stem cell research. This led to the establishment of the California Institute for Regenerative Medicine (CIRM), which has embarked on a ten-year project to bring stem cells from theory to therapy.

Conclusion

Thomas B. Okarma of Geron states the potential of regenerative medicine. "The potential for these cells is to allow permanent repair of failing organs by injecting healthy functional cells developed from them, an approach called regenerative medicine. The significance would be to broaden the definition of medical therapy from simply halting the progression of acute or chronic disease to include restoration of lost organ function."[9]

The science of stem cells holds out great promise. But to-date it is only a promise. After achieving the isolation and characterization of the first pluripotent human embryonic stem cell lines, very few additional thresholds have been crossed. No therapies have yet been developed. What we have is an investment in the future, a possible but not yet actualized future. Billions of dollars are being invested on the prospect that this is a potential future that will some day be actualized.

2.

Framing the Public Discussion of Stem Cell Ethics

In the spring of 1996, two years before James Thomson first isolated and characterized pluripotent human embryonic stem cells, Michael D. West approached myself and my colleagues at the Graduate Theological Union in Berkeley. In particular, he sought conversation with Professor Karen Lebacqz and then-doctoral student, Suzanne Holland, along with me and colleagues at the GTU's Center for Theology and the Natural Sciences. West was then CEO of the Geron Corporation; and he would be the one to take the pioneering lead in the search for "immortal lines" of regenerating cells. West wanted counsel from theologians about the ethics of stem cell research.

This little historical fact is quite significant. At no point can one say that the science was proceeding without a connection with ethics, and we mean ethics grounded in theological reflection. Public ethical discussion is open and exploratory, to be sure; but research scientists as well as policymakers have from the beginning been seeking out theological input.

Theological reflection and moral deliberation are requested by the public square

"Stem cell researchers have been confronted with the most serious religious and ethical challenge to science since the debate around nuclear fission," writes Laurie Zoloth. "In the largely secular pluralistic world of the academic science community, one is led to ask: Why do religious and philosophical arguments so dominate the debate on stem cells?"[1] To this question about the public policy debate over stem cells, what follows will provide an answer.

One fascinating element in public policy discussion over stem cells is that religious voices are being heard. The opinion of theologians is being asked for. However, the way theological opinions are received by scientists and by public policy makers differs from the way they are received in the church. Within the church, what theologians say is assumed to carry some authority. Because the Bible is an authority, and because theologians interpret the Bible, the words of theologians might be considered the Word of God, at least indirectly.

Not so in the secular public arena. In the public arena a wide variety of religious opinions is solicited. Not only Christian theologians are consulted. So also are spokespersons for Judaism, Islam, Buddhism, Hinduism, and native religious traditions.

The public square is pluralistic. Theologians are invited to speak, but not with authority. What theologians say about ethical matters is considered to be their perspective, their opinion. Even if theological opinions are taken seriously, they are not taken by themselves as definitive.

For those ethicists who think of the church as a community of theological reflection and *moral deliberation*, this should come as good news. Within the churches, topics such as stem cell research could be diagnosed and prescriptions tendered. Once this moral deliberation has reached some level of maturity, then it could be shared with scientists and the wider public. Such careful reflection and deliberation would be welcome in the public square.

This is true in principle. And sometimes it is true in practice. However, all is not peaceful in the laboratory or the public square. Unfortunately, some religious mouths have shot off their opinions before the requisite period of theological reflection and careful moral deliberation. Ethical voices have sounded like moral machine guns, blazing through the public square, cutting down the innocent as they go about their work. Ethical terrorists strike fear into the hearts of scientists in their laboratories. Researchers understandably defend themselves by hiding and avoiding dangerous public zones.

On the one hand, the new and complex science requires theological reflection and moral deliberation at the same level of newness and complexity.

Scientists as well as public policymakers were at first welcoming of religious contributions at this level. On the other hand, ethical terrorists have so shot up the public square with premature judgments accompanied by claims to apodictic authority that apply only within the church and not without, that many of those in science and in politics have fled the scene.

Be that as it may, our time calls for integrity on the part of our churches' theologians and ethicists. It calls for a period of gathering the facts, assessing what has been gathered, ferreting out implications for understanding human nature within creation and before God, and then proceeding to provide moral guidance in such a way that healthy-minded persons can find an appropriate path to follow. Robert Benne grasps the church's opportunity and accompanying responsibility to speak to the wider social order: "The church should provide a vision of the common good that is both hopeful and realistic."[2]

Unfortunately, competing ethical frameworks are non-compossible

The lingering smoke in the public square due to the firings of ethicists' guns leads to moral confusion. Boston College's Lisa Sowle Cahill sniffs the smoke. "Public debate sometimes seems to be caught in an impasse between the value of embryos and the promised benefits of stem cell research."[3] So also does Harvard's Ann Kiessling and colleague Scott Anderson. "The people with the most to gain are those patients who are sick or dying from one of the diseases targeted by stem cell therapy. For them the long-windedness of the debate is often unbearable."[4] Can we simply fire shots at all the theologians? "There are simply too many diametrically opposed theologies—many claiming to be the actual word of God—to reach a consensus."[5] Now, this is the smoke of confusion. In what follows, I hope some of the smoke will clear.

I submit that we have confusing smoke because it appears that ethicists are engaged in a public shoot-out like Wyatt Earp at the OK Corral. It was on October 26, 1881, in Tombstone, Arizona Territory, that Wyatt Earp, his brothers Morgan and Virgil along with Doc Holiday, shot at their enemies Billy Clanton and Frank and Tom McLaury. These enemies shot at each other. Could this be an analogue to today's ethical shootout? No. A closer look will show that today's ethical gunslingers are fighting in separate corrals. Only a few stray bullets now and then take a victim.

How best can we describe the current debate over stem cells? I recommend that we think of the separate corrals as separate ethical frameworks. Each framework provides a set of theological assumptions regarding human nature and regarding ethical goals. Within these frameworks moral deliberation takes place. The development of moral guidance rises up to articulation, but their respective contexts remain co-present, so to speak. What is said (*das Gesagte*) cannot be extricated from what is unsaid (*das Ungesagte*), to call to mind the hermeneutics of philosopher Hans-Georg Gadamer.

These frameworks of the unsaid are non-compossible. To be compossible, ethical frameworks would have to be compatible, consistent with one another. But they are not. They operate with different pictures of the human condition and different understandings of the central ethical question. The result is that discussants in the public conversation talk past one another. They do not engage. Or, to use our gunfight analogy, shots fired miss their targets by a mile.

Now, within each framework one could imagine a moral argument that would support stem cell research and a moral argument that would oppose it. The framework provides the background assumptions within which moral reasoning takes place. Having said this, however, each of the three frameworks we will diagnose has become identified with one or another moral position. As we will see shortly, embryo protection and nature protection have become identified with the anti-stem cell camp. The medical benefits framework has become identified with support for stem cells and the larger program of regenerative medicine.

What are the ethical frameworks in the stem cell debate?

According to my diagnosis and that of my Berkeley colleagues who have been working on this, the three non-compossible frameworks within which the current public controversy over stem cell research is being argued are these: (1) the *embryo protection* framework, (2) the *nature protection* framework, and (3) the *medical benefits* framework. Within each framework one may argue either in favor of or against support for stem cell research, even though the first two are dominated by opponents and the third by advocates.

Those firing from within the embryo protection corral are deputies of the Vatican and, in America, their evangelical allies. During the era of the George Bush administration, the White House operated from within this ethical framework. The central question of this framework is this: is human embryonic stem cell research a form of abortion? Vatican Catholics and American evangelicals answer yes. Because they have taken a previous stand against elective abortion, they feel they must commit themselves to shutting down this kind of scientific research. The destruction of the blastocyst constitutes the destruction of a human individual, or at least a potential human person. This is immoral. Scientists are dubbed "baby-killers." Stem cell scientists promote the "culture of death," to use the words of Pope John Paul II. Although stem cell research on adult stem cells could be deemed moral, research on hES cells is uncompromisingly immoral.

In the nature protection corral we find philosophers and social critics who have been opposing various forms of genetic science since the 1970s.

The fight against stem cell research extends battles fought earlier against recombinant DNA, germline intervention, the Human Genome Project, gene patenting, and cloning. The fundamental question of this framework is this: will the manipulation of human genes dehumanize us? The correlate questions are these: does the manipulation of human genes constitute Promethean *hubris* on the part of our scientists? Do scientists exhibit excessive pride by trying to make nature better? Do scientists risk violating our inherited genetic essence? Are scientists playing God? Would success at altering human nature by extending the human life span and such changes risk placing our society on a downward slippery slope toward the feared *Brave New World*, originally described in 1931 by Aldous Huxley?

When nature protectionists articulate their moral position, they say no to scientists who want to get into our DNA with wrenches and screwdrivers and try to make it better. Attempts to improve human life through genetic manipulation risk a violent response on the part of nature. They risk so violating nature that we will eventually suffer from this loss of our inherited essence. So go the arguments of those who oppose "playing God" in the laboratory. This includes, among many others, Leon Kass, former chair of the U.S. President's Council on Bioethics (COB).

The third corral has a sign on it: "Medical Benefits." Those in this ethical framework begin with the question: could regenerative medicine provide

FRAMEWORK	Embryo Protection	Nature Protection	Medical Benefits
ADVOCACY GROUPS	Vatican Catholics Evangelical Protestants Orthodox Christians	President's Council on Bioethics	Patient Advocacy Groups
SPOKESPERSONS	White House	Leon Kass, Jeremy Rifkin	All Jewish and most Christian theologians
CRITERION	Abortion Nonmalificence	Post-Human Technoscience Nonmalificence	Medical Benefits Beneficence

Three Ethical Frameworks

a leap forward in the relief of human suffering and the enhancement of human flowering; and, if so, is this opportunity a sufficient moral warrant for supporting stem cell research? What frames the moral reasoning here is the presence among us of millions if not billions of persons who suffer from genetic-based diseases or traumas such as heart disease, Parkinson's, Alzheimer's, spinal cord injury, diabetes, and others. When an opportunity to relieve suffering arises, the public policy question arises: should we muster resources for the possibility that we might be able to help large numbers of persons in dramatically decisive ways? Within the medical benefits framework we find advocates for stem cell research among our scientists and patient advocacy groups. We also find Christian and Jewish leaders who see public support as a social expression of love and justice.

These three are theologically or at least philosophically grounded ethical frameworks. There is a fourth. The fourth might be called the *research standards framework*. One might think of this as a secular framework, because it is shared by both public policy makers and laboratory researchers around the world. It spells out which procedures are deemed ethical, and in some cases even legal. It provides the criteria to meet when applying for grant funding. Frequently, a look at research standards through a magnifying glass will discern underlying theological decisions, hidden beneath secular or religiously neutral language.

In the chapters that follow, we will take a closer look at each of the three theologically based frameworks as well as the research standards framework.

3.

The Embryo Protection Framework

The National Council of the Churches of Christ in the USA frames the ethical questions surrounding stem cell research this way: "As with the abortion debate, much of the stem cell debate turns on the differing views we hold on the moral status of human embryos."[1] From the point of view of the NCC, the ethical focus is on the embryo, not the persons who might benefit from regenerative medicine. This is the basic orientation that distinguishes the *embryo protection framework*.

Ethicists within the embryo protection framework focus on the issue: does the embryo at the blastocyst stage outside a mother's body require protection from death at the hands of laboratory researchers?[2] Or, to say it another way: is stem cell research a form of abortion; and, if so, are laboratory scientists baby-killers?

As the reader can see, the targets of ethical concern here are not the potential patients who might benefit from regenerative medicine but rather the potential persons whose lives will be aborted in the petri dish. The central question deals with derivation, not benefit. The decisive issue is the moral status of the preimplantation embryo—the *ex vivo* blastocyst in the petri dish—from which human embryonic stem cells are derived. The orienting ethical question of this first framework is this: does the blastocyst have morally protectable dignity and, if so, are we are forbidden to dismantle it when pursuing medical research? One may answer yes or no to this question. The very posing of this question places the discussion within the embryo protection framework.

Opposition to stem cell research on the grounds that it is a form of abortion is most frequently associated with the Vatican, but is shared by many American evangelicals and Orthodox ethicists as well. Opposition to stem cells can be expected from the magazine *Christianity Today*, from denominations such as the Southern Baptist Convention or the Lutheran Church—Missouri Synod, as well as conservative political advocacy groups such as the "Center for Bioethics and Culture" network and "First Do No Harm."[3] Because of the worldwide attention given to the official Roman Catholic voice, this framework is often taken to be *the* religious framework.

What are the theological assumptions in the embryo protection framework?

Several key theological assumptions define those who oppose embryonic stem cell research based on moral reasoning from within the embryo protection framework. The fundamental theological assumption is that human dignity is fully established at conception; and this applies equally to zygotes both within the mother's body *in vivo* and *ex vivo* in the laboratory. What makes a human being a person is origin. Our origin at conception establishes our individuality, our dignity, and our moral protectibility.

Roman Catholic theologians offer the most complete description of this theological anthropology. What happens according to nature within a mother's body is the meeting of three things: the mother's egg, the father's sperm, and God's newly created soul. According to the late Pope John Paul II, when the sperm and egg unite to create a unique genome, then God creates an immortal spiritual soul and imparts it to the conceptus. Once the early embryo has its immortal soul, it then gains dignity. With dignity, we must protect it from destruction by medical scientists, even when it appears outside the mother's body in a laboratory setting.

What impresses the Vatican is genomic novelty. Because the genome of the conceptus is neither that of the mother nor that of the father, but rather a brand new combination of the two, this gives it individuality. Only a human individual can receive a spiritual soul; and this individuality is established at conception.

Now, we might ask, does God impart this immortal and spiritual soul promptly for the zygote while still at the single cell stage? Can we specify the exact moment of ensoulment? No, says the Vatican. Ensoulment cannot be discerned by science. It can be discerned only by philosophy. Ensoulment is metaphysical, not physical.

Does this mean the early embryo might make it to the blastocyst stage and still not have received its soul? Yes. If so, might it then be dismantled for use in stem cell research? No. Even if the soul is not yet present, it is still on the way. Once the unique genome has been established and an embryonic individual has been established, then the early embryo is ready for ensoulment. This potential for ensoulment or potential for person-hood is sufficient to confer upon the blastocyst dignity and, thereby, moral protectability. In sum, potential ensoulment is sufficient to confer dig-nity and, thereby, to block human embryonic stem cell research.

The *genomic novelty position* was articulated already in the 1987 encyclical *Donum Vitae,* directed by the head of the Congregation for the Doctrine of the Faith.[4] That director was Cardi-nal Joseph Ratzinger, now Pope Benedict XVI. This predates both the isolation of hES cells as well as the cloning of Dolly. Yet, what is said in 1987 continues to structure the Vatican position. *Donum Vitae* asserts that three elements are cru-cial to the creation of a morally defensible human individual: the father's sperm, the mother's egg, and a divinely implanted soul. *Donum Vitae* notes that at fertilization a novel genetic code—neither

that of the mother nor that of the father—is created. *Donum Vitae* takes this genomic novelty to
be evidence of the presence of a unique individual,
and thus reasonably the condition for ensoulment.
Ensoulment is the event which establishes a divine
moral claim, so that the destruction of the blastocyst constitutes not only murder but an offense
against God's creation. Once a unique genome has
been established, then it is morally incumbent on
us to protect it from harm.

Pope John Paul II was a champion of human
dignity. He defended dignity in the face of what
he perceived to be a global "culture of death."[5]
By "dignity" he meant what the Enlightenment
since Immanuel Kant has meant, namely, each
human person should be treated as a moral end
and not merely as means to some further end.
When it comes to stem cell research, to sacrifice
a future person at the blastocyst stage is to violate that early embryo's dignity. When U.S. President George W. Bush visited the Vatican in the
spring of 2001, the pope extended application of
the culture of death to include scientists research-
ing. Even though medical advance is itself a good
thing, said the Holy Father, protection of the early
embryo takes moral precedence. Our first ethical
responsibility is to do no harm—to embrace nonmaleficence—toward the unborn.

To summarize the Vatican argument, the
sequence from theological anthropology to moral
reasoning goes like this: (a) the establishment of
an individual person through genomic novelty;

(b) divine impartation of an immortal spiritual soul, or at least the potential for receiving such a soul; (c) the establishment of dignity, meaning that the early embryo should be treated as an end and not merely a means to the further end of medical research; (d) moral protectability from *ex vivo* destruction at the blastocyst stage; and, finally, (e) opposition to human embryonic stem cell research and therapy.

Some non-Catholics hold the Vatican position

Many non-Catholics rely upon the same basic moral reasoning. One Orthodox bioethicist, John Breck, reiterates the Vatican assumption with complete reliance on the principle of genomic novelty. In a statement on "Orthodoxy and Abortion," he writes, "The Orthodox Church has always taught that human life begins at conception, when a sperm unites with an ovum to produce a genetically unique living being."[6] Genetically unique human beings should be protected from abortion. It would follow that genetically unique embryos in the petri dish should be similarly protected.

Evangelical Nigel Cameron of the Center for Bioethics and Culture rests his case on "human life with a dignity which is intrinsic and, therefore, with an inalienable moral standing." This permits extension of the abortion debate to early embryo research and other "issues of life and death *ex utero*."[7] Missouri Synod Lutheran bioethicist Gilbert Meilaender supports the Vatican position as well. With dramatic appeal, he writes, "The embryo is, I believe, the weakest and least advantaged of our fellow human beings." Then, citing Karl Barth, Meilaender adds, "And no community is 'really strong if it will not carry its . . . weakest members.'"[8]

In its "Resolution: On Human Embryonic and Stem Cell Research," the Southern Baptist Convention reiterates its opposition to abortion and then calls "upon the United States Congress to maintain the existing ban on the use of tax dollars to support research which requires the destruction of human embryos."[9]

It is important to recognize that the position taken by the Vatican and its friends within the embryo protection framework is characterized by the bioethical principle of *nonmaleficence*—it ethically frames the stem cell debate as a matter of avoiding doing harm. Regardless of what good might result for future suffering persons who might benefit from today's research, the issue of doing harm or avoiding harm to the embryo takes precedence.

When we remind ourselves of the ancient Hippocrates, who still inspires modern medicine, we recall he said to benefit, and do no harm."[10] Nonmaleficence picks up on the second half of his admonition. Another bioethical principle picks up on the first half, *beneficence*, which means we should pursue better health when the opportunity is open to us. Within the embryo protection framework, nonmaleficence trumps beneficence.

Can embryo protectionists approve use of discarded or spare embryos?

What about the discarded or spare embryos sitting in freezers of IVF clinics? It is estimated that from 400,000 to 500,000 of these fertilized ova will never be implanted in a mother's body. Eventually, they will deteriorate and be destroyed. Might we benefit by thawing some of these out and using them for stem cell research? Could this be deemed moral from within the embryo protection framework?

The yes answer could be identified as the *discarded embryo* position. Some refer to it as the *nothing is lost* position. To date, the preponderance of embryonic stem cell research has been conducted on these "excess" or "surplus" or "spare" embryos originally created for purposes of in vitro fertilization. In the U.S. and United Kingdom a half million such embryos exist in storage freezers. Those who hold the discarded embryo position believe it is morally licit to use for research embryos that will otherwise be destroyed. What is illicit would be the deliberate creation of embryos that would be destroyed for research purposes. Yale theologian Gene Outka draws a conclusion: "The creation of embryos for research purposes only should be resisted, yet research on 'excess' embryos is permissible."[11] Addressing the U.S. Senate in 2005, Senator Bill Frist said, "We should federally fund research only on embryonic stem cells derived from blastocysts left over from fertility therapy, which will not be implanted or adopted but instead were otherwise destined by the parents with absolute certainty to be discarded and destroyed."[12]

Not all Roman Catholics are satisfied with the discarded embryo alternative. It looks too much like a compromise on their absolute claim. In fact, taking the Roman Catholic argument back a step, no church approval of IVF was ever given. Nor was church approval ever given of storing unused fertilized ova. IVF violates natural law; and the storing of frozen ova risks the death of potential human persons. Discarding frozen ova is a form of abortion. So when scientists take advantage of discarded or spare embryos, they are complicit in the earlier illicit act of creating zygotes that might never be brought through a pregnancy to birth. Pressing such spare zygotes into medical service does not redeem the scientists from complicity in baby-killing. Richard Doerflinger, spokesperson for the U.S. Conference of Catholic Bishops, holds this extreme view. He would say, "Intentional destruction of innocent human life at any stage is inherently evil, and no good consequence can mitigate that evil."[13]

What about the Orthodox? H. Tristram Engelhardt, Jr., an Orthodox bioethicist, defends the discarded embryo alternative with careful argumentation. The use of discarded embryos stored in IVF clinics is morally licit, because such use draws something good out of an otherwise immoral situation. "There is no bar in principle against using for a good end something that has been acquired by heinous means, as long as one has not been involved in (1) employing these evil means, (2) encouraging their use, (3) avoiding their condemnation, or (4) giving scandal through their use. One can drink water from a well that was dug by unjustly forced labor."[14]

Engelhardt's own church bishops in the Orthodox Church of America, however, would disagree. The use of discarded embryos is illicit because the original wrong of killing a potential person cannot be redeemed when the remains are pressed into medical service. "The very act of destroying those embryos is evil, and we may not profit from evil even to achieve a good and noble end."[15]

These theological deliberations have spawned secular counterparts in the research ethics framework. It has become important to both U.S. federal guidelines as well as National Academy of Sciences guidelines that embryos not be created specifically for research. Research embryos must be created for some other purpose and then diverted into research. If one asks why, no scientific reasoning can explain such a policy. The above theological reasoning is the hidden explanation underlying the secular formulations.

Could adult stem cells provide pluripotency?

Many among the embryo protectionists argue that human embryonic stem cells are unnecessary. Scientists can get what they want, namely, pluripotency and plasticity, from adult stem cells. If we could harvest adult stem cells from cord blood or nerves or other sources, then no blastocysts would need to be destroyed. Scientists could pursue regenerative medicine without becoming baby-killers.

Roman Catholic bioethicists are the ones most likely to lift up the prospect that adult stem cell use will make hES cell use unnecessary. "The progress and results obtained in the field of adult stem cells (ASC) show not only their great plasticity but also their many possible uses, in all likelihood no different from those of embryonic stem cells."[16]

Unfortunately, as we saw in the earlier chapter on the science of stem cells, this is not scientifically possible. Adult stem cells are in some cases multipotent, but this is insufficient. Multipotent cells are already destined to remain within their own already differentiated type. And, what is decisive, multipotent stem cells lack the plasticity to integrate into the host tissue. Adult stem cells "do not prove true stem cell plasticity."[17] Research on the medical value of adult stem cells should continue, certainly; but they cannot become a replacement for pluripotent hES cells. This attempt to circumvent the ethical challenge by sidestepping blastocyst disaggregation lacks scientific support.

Just when does an individual appear?

Before we look at more differences in moral reasoning within the embryo protection framework, let us return for a moment to the relevant science. Should the Vatican or John Breck rely on the concept of genomic novelty as the requisite for ensoulment and personhood in the way they do?

Other options are available. Traditional Jews date ensoulment at quickening, 40 days after conception. According to the Qur'an, Muslims can appeal to either 40 or 120 days after conception. In both cases, ensoulment takes place within the mother's body. It would not take place in a laboratory petri dish.

Identifying ensoulment with the establishment of a unique genome is questionable, because nothing like an individual person appears in early embryogenesis either in the petri dish or the mother's body. At the moment of conception a unique genome is established, to be sure. However, this is not the moment in which a new individual person is created. Nor is it the case that each new human person possesses a single unique genome. The science can be helpful here.

Three phenomena are well worth paying attention to. First, the mother's body does not necessarily honor the moment in which a unique genome is established with quite the respect the ethicists do. Estimates range from 50 percent to 80 percent of naturally fertilized eggs are flushed from the mother's body before they can adhere to the uterine wall. Ponder just how many unique genomes get flushed right out of the system! If the Vatican is serious about associating a divine soul with each and every zygote, and if the mother's body by nature eliminates the majority of ensouled embryos, then theologically it would be difficult to see God's intentions as carried out by natural processes.

The second relevant phenomenon is twinning. The zygote is preformed. Each cell for a number of days is totipotent—that is, each blastomere can make an entire person, at least in principle. During the first few days the bunch of cells can divide into twins, quadruplets, or rarely octuplets. Each of these individuals would have the same genetic code. Monozygotic twins—what we call "identical" twins—are the result of such cell division. If identical triplets are born, we know that the early embryo had split into four and one of them was flushed from the mother's body at some point. Further, during these early stages, which can last up to 12 or 14 days, these divided embryos can recombine. Twins can become a single person again. All this is possible because the cells that are dividing during early embryo development are preformed, not yet differentiated, not yet committed to making one or more individual human beings. We must conclude that nature does not connect genetic uniqueness with the uniqueness of being a human individual.

The third phenomenon of interest is chimerism. A chimera is a single individual with two or more genomes. Within the mother's body, *in vivo*, frequently two or more eggs can be fertilized at the same time. If two separate fertilized eggs develop simultaneously and each creates its own pregnancy, two babies will be born at the same time. We know these as "fraternal" twins—that is, twins with different genomes. Fraternal twins are the equivalent of any other pair of brothers and sisters. Yet—and here is the interesting point—this pair of zygotes can combine to form a single embryo. If brought to term, the resulting baby is a chimera, a single person with two genetic codes.

Now it gets even more fascinating. If the two fertilized ova are of the same gender, then the baby girl or baby boy may grow up, live a normal life, and never know that he or she began as fraternal twins. If, however, a male and female combine, then the resulting baby is a hermaphrodite. The term "hermaphrodite" combines the names of two Greek gods, the male Hermes with the female Aphrodite. Doctors may look at such a newborn baby and wonder, "Now, just what is it? A boy? A girl?" Frequently early surgery steers the newborn in the direction of one gender or the other. In such a case, a genetic test is likely to reveal two genomes, one with a Y chromosome and the other with two Xs.

One conclusion we might draw from these phenomena is this: if it is important that ensoulment and dignity belong to a single individual with a single genome, then nothing like this can be established at conception *in vivo*, let alone at the blastocyst stage *ex vivo*. Perhaps the 14-day rule might take this discussion a bit further.

Might the 14-day rule
offer a compromise?

If we would like to press the theological logic tied to the human individual, adherence to the uterine wall accompanied by the appearance of the primitive streak between 12 and 14 days stand up and ask for notice. Conservative Roman Catholic bioethicist Norman Ford has taken notice. "In short, it can be argued," says Ford, "the presence of the genetic code itself does not suffice to constitute a human individual, but that only its activation does, whereby specialized cells and membranes are produced to form and enclose an organized human individual about fourteen days after fertilization. If this argument is accepted, fertilization is not the beginning of the development *of* the human individual but the beginning of the formative process and development *into* one (or more human individuals). Ultimately this issue cannot be resolved in the first instance by appealing to the teaching of the Church, but only by reflection and critical analysis on all the relevant scientific information interpreted in the light of sound philosophical principles."[18]

Ford is trying to find a compromise path the Vatican can follow. Not everyone is so patient. Impatient with those who seek to block stem cell research by protecting the early embryo, Ann Kiessling and Scott Anderson weigh in, supporting the 14-day rule as the minimum threshold for establishing individuality. "The moment when a

sperm and an egg meet provides a romantic start-
ing point for life, but in reality that moment is
pretty fuzzy . . . conception fails as a signpost for
novel life. It is also clear that not every zygote is
destined by nature to complete the journey. Along
the way, problems may occur that cause up to
two-thirds of all zygotes to be lost. . . . Until about
day 14, the blastocyst has the potential to split
and form twins. The idea of personhood before
this time is counterintuitive."[19]

In principle, one could use this emphasis on
individuation at 14 days to support opposition
to abortion as well as support research on hES
cells. If we understand opposition to abortion as
the removal of a fetus from a pregnant woman's
body, one could take a pro-life stand on abortion
and still affirm that human embryonic stem cell
research is morally licit. Ford himself does not follow this path; but it is a reasonable one to take,
given Ford's reasoning.

Let us pause for just a moment to compare the
abortion debate that broke out in the late 1960s with
the contemporary stem cell debate. Commonly we
would define elective abortion as the surgical removal
of a fetus from a woman's body. Stem cell research
does not involve the removal of a fetus from a woman's body. What laboratory scientists are interested
in is the blastocyst at four to six days. Even *in vivo*,
the blastocyst would not be adhering to the mother's
uterine wall. These are notable differences.

The focus of opposition between pro-choice
and pro-life arguments in the abortion debate is

the woman's right to choose. This does not apply
to *ex vivo* research, at least not after her decision
to donate her genetic material to science. What
needs to be spelled out within the embryo protection framework is just how and how not the stem
cell debate represents a reiteration of the abortion
debate.

Arguing in support of stem cells from within the embryo protection framework

Recall that within the Vatican position we could
distinguish between potential ensoulment and
actual ensoulment. For the two recent popes,
potential ensoulment is sufficient to establish
dignity and moral protectability. On the basis of
potential ensoulment or even potential personhood, might the logic go the opposite direction?

A potential person is not an actual person.
Potential dignity is not actual dignity. Might we
find room here for use of *ex vivo* blastocysts in
medical research? Karen Lebacqz thinks so. She
puts it this way: "First, the embryo or tissue must
be valued. . . . To respect the embryo is to affirm
that the value of the embryo or tissue is *not* dependent on its value for us or its usefulness to us.
Respect sees a value in itself beyond usefulness.
. . . Second, such an entity can be used in research
and can even be killed. To do so is not in itself
disrespectful."[20]

In parallel fashion, Roman Catholic bioethicist Thomas Shannon gingerly works through the

issues to find a way to meet the Vatican concerns to protect human dignity while recognizing an opening toward stem cell research. Right after fertilization, Shannon grants, the zygote is a living entity. It possesses human nature. But this is a *common* human nature with an array of potentials. Even if personhood is one of the potentials, the activated zygote is not yet an individuated person; and thus it does not yet have dignity. Embryogenesis is a process, and dignity cannot be applied until we have an individual person. Individuation does not appear at conception, as the Vatican mistakenly assumes. "Persons," Shannon argues, "have a dignity; natures have a value. The dignity of the person grounds a more absolute standing. . . . The value of human nature does not generate the same level of protection. . . . Nonetheless, it is human nature and it is to be valued."[21] In sum, one can hold a position that affirms an early embryo is a person in potential and, with an appropriate level of respect, still support embryonic stem cell research.

Gilbert Meilaender, whom we associated with a stricter embryo protection position above, finds such arguments for respect or value ascribed to the pre-differentiated embryo less than convincing. He recommends that, "If we forge ahead with embryonic stem cell research, we simply scrap the language of respect or profound respect for those embryos that we create and discard according to our purposes. Such language does not train us to think seriously about the choices we are making, and it is, in any case, not likely to be believed."[22]

Meilaender is among those who would take a position contrary to that of Lebacqz and Shannon. Meilaender argues that the embryo–though obviously not a human being in the full sense–is still at minimum a *potential* human being; and this potentiality warrants protection. The blastocyst should not be treated as a means to some further end; to do so would be to ignore the continuous development of the individual from the embryonic to fetal and infant stages. It follows that human embryonic stem cell research should be halted. Meilaender can find support from Roman Catholic Lisa Sowle Cahill, who says, "The counterargument is that as long as an embryo is a developing life within a human genetic code, it is a person despite its uncertain identity and prospects."[23]

Conclusion

Within the embryo protection framework, one might argue against stem cell research or in favor of research. Either way, the focal question has to do with the moral status of the *ex vivo* blastocyst. The central ethical concern here is nonmaleficence–that is, how to avoid doing harm to the early embryo. When we turn to the nature protection and medical benefits frameworks, we will see that moral reasoning pivots on a different center.

4.

The Nature Protection Framework

The central question that orients the *nature protection framework* is this: are scientists manipulating the genetic nature of human beings to such an extent that they "play God" and risk hurling our society down a path toward a *Brave New World*? To this question one could, in principle, answer yes or no. Critics of stem cell research answer yes.

When opponents to stem cell research and similar research into genetics speak, one can hear frequent references to Prometheus, Frankenstein, pride, *hubris*, and disdain for the so-called technoscientific or post-human future. The appeal to nature protection can be recognized with its slogan descriptors, such as "anti-Brave New World" or "anti-playing God."

Arguments against geneticists from within this framework rise up out of a stew pot of fear. The fear at work here is that the human race is being hoodwinked by a conspiracy of mad scientists and their paid ethicists to sacrifice what is precious about human nature while promoting a post-human future. Human nature is under threat; and we must protect it!

From what do we need protection? The threat comes from the de-humanizing forces of technology. Almost nobody openly advocates creating a *Brave New World* as depicted in Aldous Huxley's novel, written in 1931. The enemy is not mounting a direct assault. Rather, the enemy is ambient. It inheres to our cultural environment. It is the culture of progress and technological advance applied to the essence of human nature. Human nature is just fine the way it is, thank you. It does not need improvement.

The anti-Brave-New-World rebels feel that they stand in opposition to an implicit worldview—what they perceive to be a dominant or prevailing worldview—over against which they need to take a stand. Lutheran theologian Philip Hefner describes this worldview. "We approach nature—including our own human nature—in terms of what we can make of it; nature is not something we accept, rather it is the object of our fantastic ability to re-shape our world. Further, this characteristic is not incidental, but it reveals itself as a fundamental American habit of the heart."[1] The American habit that opponents to a brave new world shun is the habit of re-shaping what nature has given us. To technologize and transform the human race into a post-human future strikes fear into the hearts of those who revere nature as it is.

The U.S. President's Council on Bioethics argues for protecting human nature

Arguments raised from within this framework have been most coherently articulated by the majority members of President George W. Bush's Council on Bioethics.[2] Consciously calling to mind the moral warnings of Huxley's famous *a Brave New World*, this framework comprehends the stem cell debate by first imagining undesirable and unforeseen consequences of stem cell research, and working backward from these undesirable futures to regulate present-day policy. Positions employing this framework usually assume a reverence for nature, an appreciation for the human plight with reproduction and disease. They fear getting too far away from what is natural.

Leon Kass, University of Chicago professor and former chair of President George W. Bush's Council of Bioethics (COB), speaks for the policymakers. When denouncing reproductive cloning, he writes, "I exaggerate somewhat, but in the direction of truth: we are compelled to decide nothing less than whether human procreation is going to remain human, whether children are going to be made to order rather than begotten, and whether we wish to say yes in principle to the road that leads to the designer hell of *Brave New World*."[3] Kass's denunciation of reproductive cloning here leads also to a correlate denunciation of therapeutic cloning—that is, a ban against stem cell research. Even if stem cell research has some redeeming features, it should be outlawed because the development of the technique for therapeutic cloning could be co-opted by those who would use it for reproductive cloning. "What we need is an all-out ban on human cloning, including the creation of embryonic clones."[4]

Nature protection requires that we avoid playing God with our genomes

To protect human nature, we must avoid playing God with our genomes, say nature protectionists. Opponents to playing God argue that while any individual case of technoscientific advance might be ethically permissible, the cumulative effects of widespread biotechnological pursuit cannot be adequately anticipated. Nature protectionists worry that human desire for technological advancement will go unbridled, confusing genetic medicine with genetic enhancement, thus producing an unjust society of genetic haves and have-nots. As such, these moralists argue that it is pride or *hubris* to believe that through science and technology we can control human biological destiny. To think that we can control human nature through genetic manipulation is to play God; and it is to risk reprisal by nature, resulting in some unimaginable tragedy.

Called to mind here is the ancient myth of Prometheus and the modern myth of Frankenstein. Leon Kass shrinks away in horror from "the Frankensteinian *hubris* to create human life and increasingly to control its destiny; man playing

God."[5] Within this framework some ethicists conclude that destruction of embryos, even in pursuit of medical benefits, risks coarsening society to the value of nascent human life; and, as such, its future risks outweigh its present benefits.

In the ancient world of the Greeks, people feared the gods of Olympus. They sought to propitiate the gods in order to ensure health and prosperity. We moderns no longer believe in such gods. In their place we have set nature. Instead of the gods, some among us believe we should revere nature. We have replaced an avoidance of acting *contra deum*, against God's will, with a new proscription against acting *contra naturam*, against nature. To avoid "playing God" means for us to avoid acting contrary to nature. What has happened is that nature has become tacitly sacred.

Implicit in the anti-playing-God position, therefore, is a reverence for nature that makes nature functionally sacred. DNA has become the icon of nature's sacredness. Assumed to be the essence or secret to life, the genetic code is lifted up by this position as quasi-holy. With their secular sacrality, the genes should be morally off-limits to science. Scientists who alter the human genome are accused of playing God, of crossing the line that led to the punishment of Prometheus by Zeus.[6]

Is there wisdom in "yuck"?

When the cloning controversy broke out with the announcement of Dolly the cloned sheep in late

February 1997, the entire world went, "yuck!" How dare scientists manipulate and violate our sacred DNA! The reaction was visceral. Reproductive cloning was immediately perceived to be a threat to human individuality, identity, and dignity. Nobody wanted it. So scientists were blamed for presenting us with this threat, a threat nobody welcomed.

What many commonly understand as the "yuck factor" is known more eruditely as "wisdom of repugnance." Leon Kass refers to "yuck" as "repugnance." Furthermore, Kass believes repugnance tells us which direction our ethics should follow. The Kass position grounds ethics in the recognition that advancing technologies can strike with visceral repugnance that belies any easy rational articulation. This repugnance functions as a moral alarm, alerting us to the potential harms of "unnatural" intervention. *Offensive, grotesque, revolting, repugnant,* and *repulsive* are the words Kass lifts up as reactions to genetic technology, specifically cloning. Such words count methodologically for Kass, because he relies upon the wisdom inherent in the emotional intuition of repugnance. "Repugnance is the emotional expression of deep wisdom, beyond reason's power fully to articulate it."[7] Genetic technoscience dehumanizes us, because it alienates us from our sense of belonging to nature.

What all this presupposes is commitment to a form of naturalism. It is not explicitly theological in that no appeal is made to divine revelation.

Yet it is implicitly theological or at least philosophical. This is because nature in the form of human DNA takes on a tacitly sacred status. What yuck or repugnance do, allegedly, is bring our deep nature up to the surface where it can play a role in public policymaking. We label the assumed position within the nature protection framework *neo-naturalism.*

Social activist Jeremy Rifkin provides a full-blown naturalism that seeks a "resacralization" of nature. Rifkin objects to "the upgrading of existing organisms and the design of wholly new ones with the intent of perfecting their performance." To protect our genetic nature from human techno-scientific intervention and modification, he trumpets: "The resacralization of nature stands before us as the great mission of the coming age."[8] Rifkin assumes that nature is good as we find it. Biotechnical interventions, such as embryonic stem cell research and regenerative medicine built on genetic modification, are violations of the moral order of nature. The ethical import of resacralizing nature is to provide moral warrant for preventing scientists from re-engineering DNA.

Laurie Zoloth suggests that this protectiveness toward mother nature is due to a vague fear that modernity is moving too quickly. Nostalgia for a disappearing past rises up within us to say, no! There are some things about nature we simply do not need to know; and certainly there are some things about nature we ought not to try to change! "Research raises fears about forbidden and new knowledge; in other ways, it potentiates fears about violations of 'mother nature', an argument engaged by both fundamentalists and environmentalists. The forbidden nature or the speed of research is part of a larger debate about modernity, its pace, and its uses."[9]

Nature protectionists, like embryo protectionists, fear a slippery slope

Embryo protectionists and nature protectionists fear that, if we permit the destruction of blastocysts for use in medical research and therapy, we will gradually lose our commitment to protect human life in general. The bishops of the Orthodox Church in America give voice to this fear. "The slippery slope . . . is dangerous and potentially irreversible. . . . The slope will lead to a tragic devaluation of human life."[10]

From within the U.S. President's Council, COB member Charles Krauthammer rings the alarm. "We will, slowly and by increments, have gone from stem cells to embryo farms to factories with fetuses hanging (metaphorically) on meat hooks waiting to be cut open and used by the already born."[11] The passion with which resistance to stem cell research rises is due in large part to the fear of the slippery slope.

Christopher Thomas Scott does not fear the slippery slope that leads from stem cell decisions ineluctably toward a Brave New World. Previous advances in medical science have not demonstrated that society allows matters to get out of control. "The *Brave New World* view argues that we stand at the precipice of a slippery slope. It contends that using blastocysts for research amounts to human commoditization, that it inevitably encourages a marketplace of embryo farms, fetuses made for spare parts and cloned human beings. I think this scenario is unlikely. . . . The steady march of humankind's medical discoveries has been overwhelmingly used for good."[12]

Some argue for regenerative medicine and other forms of technoscience

Ann Kiessling and Scott Anderson would like to see stem cell science move forward; and this makes them impatient with nature protectionists who accuse researchers of playing God or acting like Frankenstein. These two blame the scientific community for this, because scientists too often hide behind the complexity of their self-descriptions. This creates an unnecessary and dangerous sense in the wider public that laboratories are mysterious and sinister places. "The usual concern is that the scientists are trying to play God, but are instead creating monsters using dark and mysterious technologies. Unfortunately, the language of the stem cell investigator is still baffling to the majority of citizens. Instead of scientists valiantly struggling to cure disease, many see Dr. Frankenstein tending his embryo farm. Scientists, having made their research inaccessible to the layperson, must shoulder some of the blame for the confusion."[13]

Still, some advocates of technoscience are in-your-face, so to speak, about transforming human nature into something beyond nature. One can find such commitments among nanotechnologists and post-humanists as well as geneticists. Stanley Shostak, for example, would give a neo-natural-ist nightmares. He contends that "a high priority should be placed on manipulating genes, fulfilling biotechnology's potential for creating a healthier and happier humanity."[14] Going beyond happiness as we have known it, Shostak will stop at nothing short of making people immortal through regen-erative gene therapy.

Although sharing this optimism of what genetic science can accomplish, Michael D. West presses us forward but with a bit more caution against a Brave New World. On the one hand, West strongly supports scientific advance in the direction of improving human health and well-being. "I actu-ally value the title of Aldous Huxley's novel *Brave New World,* for we need to make a new world—not the world of Aldous Huxley's novel, but a world free of the scourges of diabetes and heart disease."[15] Yet, on the other hand, West opposes genetic enhancement and, thereby, opposes a post-human future. "My nightmare is that the *hubris* of some scientists would have us engineer-ing *people* from genetically modified cells. Their goal is 'enhancement', to make 'superpeople', individuals better than any living on the planet today."[16] Making superpeople is West's nightmare, not dream. Although there may be a threat to our humanity lurking in genetic science, West is convinced that the threat is not coming from human embryonic stem cell research.

Nonmaleficence orients the nature protection framework

It is worth noting that, like the embryo protection framework, the nature protection framework portrays the stem cell debate primarily in terms of nonmaleficence. Accordingly, our primary moral responsibility is to guard against the potential negative consequences of biotechnological research. In this framework ethicists wish to avoid doing harm to our DNA and to our culture; whereas the embryo protectionists wish to avoid doing harm to the blastocyst.

In summary, the nature protection framework is an application of the widespread fear that advancing technology risks divorcing our consciousness as human beings from our biological embeddedness in the natural realm. More frequently than not, positions taken within this framework partner themselves with the embryo protectionists. This certainly has been the case with President George W. Bush, whose COB gives voice to both nature protection and embryo protection.

5.

The Medical Benefits Framework

When in 2004 California voters passed Proposition 71—the California Stem Cell Research and Cures Initiative—the motive was clear: to help cure people from suffering. The ballot measure began: "Millions of children and adults suffer from devastating diseases or injury that are currently incurable, including cancer, diabetes, heart disease, Alzheimer's, Parkinson's, spinal cord injuries, blindness, Lou Gehrig's Disease, HIV/AIDS, mental health disorders, multiple sclerosis, Huntington's disease, and more than 70 other disease and injuries."[1] The measure went on to authorize $295 million in bond sales per year for ten years to fund stem cell research, all in the hope that this form of medical science could bring the human race less suffering in the future. This measure was developed within the *medical benefits framework* of ethical deliberation.

Recall that the embryo protection and nature protection frameworks orient themselves around the bioethical principle of nonmaleficence—that is, toward avoiding harm to either the embryo or to our human nature. Nonmaleficence belongs to part of Hippocrates's admonition to benefit and do no harm. As we turn to the medical benefits framework, it is the other principle that moves front and center, namely, beneficence. The ethical targets are those persons, perhaps numbering in the billions on our planet, who suffer from diseases or traumas that regenerative medicine could help.[2]

The orienting ethical questions within the medical benefits framework include the following: if regenerative medicine could provide a leap forward in the relief of human suffering and the enhancement of human flowering, does this provide sufficient moral warrant for supporting stem cell research? Should society muster resources now in order to benefit those who will be suffering a half-generation from now? Should we see medical scientists as agents of God's creative and redemptive work?

We find many Jewish thinkers saying yes. They argue that the pursuit of medical science is itself a religious responsibility. The religious responsibility position can be found among Jewish ethicists who rely on the concept of *tikkun olam*—the responsibility to join God in repairing and transforming a broken world. Similarly, many Christian theologians and ethicists appeal to the concept of *agape*—understood as the responsibility to love one's neighbor. Virtually all Jewish ethicists work from within the medical benefits framework; and many Christian thinkers do as well.

Christian theologians working within this framework believe that God intends abundance or "fullness" of life for all (John 3:16). Although this "gospel in miniature," as Martin Luther described this passage, uses the word *eternal* to describe life, it carries the connotation of "abundant" or "flourishing" life. Because our life in Christ is eternal, our temporal life becomes abundant.

With this in mind, advocates of regenerative medicine within the medical benefits camp focus on the revolutionary therapeutic potential represented by stem cell research. As we have repeated many times, stem cells hold out hope of developing therapies for persons suffering from cancer, spinal injury, heart disease, macular degeneration, diabetes, Parkinson's, Alzheimer's, and countless other diseases that devastate many in our population. If science in the form of regenerative medical research can give expression to Christian compassion for those who suffer, and can serve human well-being and flourishing, if not abundance, this is moral warrant to do so. To support science in this enterprise is an act of society's stewardship. It supports a God-given potential for the benefit of this world.

Jewish theology and bioethics categorically supports regenerative medical research

All Jewish organizations that have officially addressed the public-policy question of stem cell research have come out supportive, even supportive of federal funding. With the tradition of *tikkun olam* as the background, Jews believe we in the human race have been invited by God to participate in the healing of the as-yet unfinished creation. "After creating man and woman, God empowered them to enter a partnership with Him in the stewardship of the world. The Torah commands us to treat and cure the ill and to defeat disease wherever possible; to do this is to be the Creator's partner in safeguarding the created."[3] Jewish tradition strongly supports the practice of medicine and, thereby, indirectly supports this kind of medical research.

More than a mere divine invitation is at stake. Actually, God places on us a duty to pursue healing, a command. Jewish bioethics is largely deontological—that is, grounded in the call to duty. "For Judaism, God owns everything, including our bodies," writes bioethicist Elliot N. Dorff. "God lends our bodies to us for this duration of our lives, and we return them to God when we die." What this implies is that "God can and does assert the right to restrict how we use our bodies."[4] This leads directly to the mandate to heal, to moral support for the practice of medicine. "Because God owns our bodies, we are required to help other people escape sickness, injury, and death."[5] Support for clinical medical practice implies, in addition, support for scientific research on behalf of human health and well being.[6]

Dorff proceeds to apply these commitments to the stem cell controversy. "The potential of stem cell research for creating organs for transplantation and cures for diseases is, at least in theory, both awesome and hopeful. Indeed, in light of our divine mandate to seek to maintain life and health, one might even contend that from a Jewish perspective we have a *duty* to proceed with that research."[7] It is our duty, based upon a command implicit in God's creation, to pursue stem cell research.

Laurie Zoloth gives voice to her response to a duty to God to heal. "We have a duty to heal, and this is expressed in legal and social policy. To turn from the possibility of healing would be an abrogation of an essential duty."[8] This recalls Rabbi Moshe David Tendler, who testified before the U.S. President's National Bioethics Advisory Commission during the Clinton administration. He said that "mastery of nature for the benefit of those suffering from vital organ failure is an obligation. Human embryonic stem cell research holds that promise."[9]

We can expect that Jewish theologians and bioethicists—virtually all Jewish intellectuals—will support regenerative medicine, including human embryonic stem cell research. As they do so, they work from within the medical benefits framework.

Jesus' ministry of healing provides a model for Christian ethics

Jesus was a healer. So also are today's medical doctors. Indirectly, so also are stem cell researchers.

Jesus forcefully taught about healing as well as demonstrating it. The Good Samaritan parable provides a vivid example. According to the New Testament, Jesus is asked by a man, "What must I do to inherit eternal life?" The man wants immortality, life in abundance. What follows is a dialogue regarding God's law. The questioner claims that he has fulfilled the law, to the letter. Yet something is missing. What is missing is compassion for the neighbor, an aggressive beneficence. To get at what is missing, Jesus tells a story. This story is instructive for us here.

"A man was going down from Jerusalem to Jericho, and fell into the hands of robbers, who stripped him, beat him, and went away, leaving him half dead. Now by chance a priest was going down that road; and when he saw him, he passed by on the other side. So likewise a Levite, when he came to the place and saw him, passed by on the other side. But a Samaritan while traveling came near him; and when he saw him, he was moved with pity. He went to him and bandaged his wounds, having poured oil and wine on them. Then he put him on his own animal, brought him to an inn, and took care of him. The next day he took out two denarii, gave them to the innkeeper, and said, 'Take care of him; and when I come back, I will repay you whatever more you spend.' Which of these three, do you think, was a neighbor to the man who fell into the hands of the robbers?" He said, "The one who showed him mercy." Jesus said to him, "Go and do likewise." (NRSV Luke 10:30-37)

Significant here is that both the priest and Levite passed by on the other side. By this passing they could pass an ethical test when nonmaleficence is the criterion. When they saw the suffering man, then did not walk over and harass him or kick him. They did not add to his misery. They were certainly ethical in this sense.

Still, Jesus lured his listener toward something more. The Samaritan felt "pity," and he acted on his pity. He found a creative way to provide help and sustenance. We ask: could the Good Samaritan provide a model for our society today? Could regenerative medicine be understood by analogy as the aid the Samaritan offered to the suffering victim? Supporters say yes.

After wondering what to do, the Samaritan elected to take the beaten man to the inn. In those days, hospitals named "Good Samaritan" had not yet been invented. The very existence in our society of hospitals named after the Good Samaritan is testimony that some have heard the call of compassion to go beyond nonmaleficence to beneficence.

Should ethics plan on making the future better than the past or present?

To make an argument in support of regenerative medicine from within the medical benefits framework coherent, ethics must be future-oriented. Beginning with a vision of a redeemed creation with an anticipated wholeness, present suffering becomes unacceptable. The biomedical sciences become a means by which one strives to realize that future vision during the present era.

The future orientation of this brand of moral reasoning fits with the future orientation of medical research. The promise of stem cell therapies still lies in the future. And it is still an uncertain future. The benefit of this research is contingent, still undetermined. Many critics who rail against mustering large sums of social capital to support regenerative medicine caution against the "hype" that is often associated with stem cells. To be realistic, this caution should be heeded. Yet also to be heeded is a reason to hope. In the place of "hype" some would put "hope"—genuine theological hope in the future. The science of regenerative medicine provides hope based on a vision of a future with improved human health and well-being.[10]

Theologically, human reality is not defined by its origin. The human race is not defined by its origin in the Book of Genesis, by the models of Adam and Eve. Nor is it defined by some moment in our evolutionary past when we emerged from the ancestry we shared in common with the primates. Rather, who we are as human beings is defined by God's appointed destiny, by our future. This includes healing. It includes healing from pain and suffering, as well as healing from the vicissitudes of death. It includes resurrection into the new creation. Just as Jesus rose from the dead, the Christian promise is that we too shall rise (1 Cor. 15:20). We can envision with the last book of the Bible, Revelation, a future life with God in which "mourning and crying and pain will be no more" (Rev. 21:4). If God promises a future transformation, then today's ethics should not be oriented toward our past origin or maintaining our inherited nature. A transformationist anthropology should lead to a transformationist ethic.

Social justice is entailed in beneficence

We know what the justice questions are. Just to remind us, Yale ethicist Margaret Farley raises the issue of justice regarding stem cell research. "Who will be expected to be the primary donors of embryos or aborted fetuses? Will gender, race, and class discrimination characterize the whole process of research on stem cells? And will the primary goals of research be skewed toward profit rather than toward healing? Who will gain from the predicted marvelous therapeutic advances achieved through stem cell research—the wealthy but not the poor? The powerful but not the marginal?"[11]

Justice is an inextricable element in the beneficence agenda. The benefits of exotic science ought not to be limited to only the wealthy who can pay large sums. Because of the cost of such expensive science, and because of the need for patenting intellectual property in order to draw financial investment, our society risks losing all the benefits of stem cell science to an economic system that favors the rich among us.

"In America, the uninsured with minimal access to basic health care continue to vex political policy," opines Laurie Zoloth. "International issues of distributive justice render the problem of access to new research and the therapies that will emerge from such research as a central ethical concern."[12]

The question of *access* looms large within the medical benefits framework. One might ask: how can we assure access to the benefits of regenerative science on the part of the poorest of the poor, regardless of where they live in this world? Smoke screens and sleights of hand on the part of investors and regulators who make big promises now must find that later, when delivery is ready, a system is in place to guarantee widespread access.

Can we accuse medical benefits advocates of utilitarianism?

It appears to critics from within the embryo protection framework that medical benefits advocates are utilitarian, that they *use* blastocysts as *means* to a further *end*. The passage cited above in the work of Laurie Zoloth could be an example. "The limited moral status of the *in vitro* blastocyst

determines duties to it, and the relatively larger
(some say unlimited) duties to the ill and vulner-
able may be primary ones. We have a duty to heal,
and this is expressed in legal and social policy. To
turn away from the possibility of healing would
be an abrogation of an essential duty."[13] Note that
Zoloth's argument is based upon an appeal to
duty toward those who suffer; it is a deontological
and not a utilitarian argument. Yet her opponents
would consider this an example of utilitarianism
or, even worse, consequentialism, in which our
unqualified duty to the unborn is allegedly subor-
dinated to a higher good.

Embryo protectionists say stem cell supporters
are in the business of making a trade-off. It is not
morally licit to trade the life of a potential person
at the blastocyst stage for speculations that other
patients might someday benefit from this kind of
science. Nonmaleficence on behalf of the early
embryo trumps beneficence on behalf of suffering
patients.

To accuse medical benefits advocates of utilitarianism puts the public policy debate into the
impasse with which we have become familiar. As
pointed out earlier when citing Lisa Sowle Cahill,
"Public debate sometimes seems to be caught in
an impasse between the value of embryos and the
promised benefits of stem cell research."[14] Now, the
impasse may at first appear to be due to utilitarianism on the part of the medical benefits advocates;
but a closer look will show that it is due to non-
compossible ethical frameworks. No one working

from within the medical benefits framework proposes that we sacrifice early human persons on behalf of laboratory experimentation and the hope of relieving the suffering of others. It is not a matter of sacrificing babies to heal grown-ups.

Defenders will argue to the contrary that a beneficence position within the medical benefits framework is not utilitarian. It does not advocate sacrificing babies for grown-ups. Conscientious ethicists in this camp would not accept just any or all means to reach a desired end, to be sure. Some acts are inherently immoral; and a just end does not justify an immoral act. Beneficence advocates do not rely on a utilitarian framework. Even Jewish bioethicist Zoloth above was answering the call to duty, the divinely ordained duty to heal.

So, to blunt the attacks of their opponents, advocates of human embryonic stem cell research must spend some effort arguing from within the embryo protection framework. Most frequently, stem cell supporters who are more at home in the medical benefits framework will appeal to the 14-day rule or a similar developmentalist position on human personhood and human dignity. They need to deny that they are baby-killers. Once the matter of the moral status of the blastocyst is settled, then regenerative medicine advocates can return to arguments based on beneficence.

Some level of moral urgency adheres to scientific research

Those supporting regenerative medicine in the medical benefits camp argue strenuously that it is immoral for us to slow down the speed of research. Every year that goes by without developing effective therapies for cancer or heart disease or Alzheimer's means another year of needless suffering and death. The countless individuals who will continue to be victims of these genetically related diseases can claim that their blood is on the hands of the embryo protectionists who were able to use public policy to shut down life-saving research.

Eric Juengst and Michael Fossel raise an argument such as this. "If ethicists or the public would restrict the uses of embryonic stem cells, then they must then bear responsibility for those patients they have chosen not to try to save by this means. Currently, patients die regularly because transplantable organs are unavailable. There is no moral culpability in this: physicians are powerless. If stem cell research can provide the power to address this need, however, the claims of those patients become compelling."[15]

Conclusion

What we have done here is to analyze three theologically based ethical frameworks within which moral positions are currently being taken in the debate over the permissibility or non-permissibility of embryonic stem cell research. In each framework, we note an implicit if not explicit commitment to protecting dignity. Whether it is the dignity of the embryo, the dignity of DNA, or the dignity of potential beneficiaries of medical research, all three frameworks presume that someone or something should be treated as an end and not utilized as a mere means.

This shared commitment to dignity demonstrates that all three positions should be considered *ethical* positions. None advocates something unethical or immoral. All want what is good and wholesome for the human race. Yet they find themselves in lively if not bitter opposition to one another. Curiously, ethically minded people can become gun fighters in moral wars and cultural wars, firing moral invectives. Each combatant believes he or she is right.

6.

The Research Standards Framework

The three ethical frameworks we have already treated share one item in common: all three are based upon recognizable theological (or philosophical, in the case of nature protection) assumptions regarding human nature and our ethical goal. One test of moral reasoning within each framework is consistency between moral decisions and the anthropological assumptions that undergird them.

Not so when we turn to the *research standards framework*. When we turn to what are becoming policies and guidelines and requirements that laboratory scientists must adhere to, we find an agglomeration of principles that do not seem to require either justification or coherence. One reason for this is that the moral reasoning behind research guidelines is frequently obscured by the translation from a theologically based framework into a secular framework. Scientists work within a secular ethical framework, which lifts up the moral standards to which they measure themselves. But the moral warrant for these standards is not articulated in the standards themselves.

In the next few years, we can expect to see moral reasoning take increasing regulatory form. This will be combined with emerging standards for quality in medical products. In the United States, the Food and Drug Administration will expand its investigations and establish new sets of standards.[1] In the meantime, we have already seen appearing in many parts of the world tentative compendia of research standards, many of which are already rising up to take at least *de facto* regulatory status.

"Ethics isn't limited to street corners, coffee shops, and university corridors," observes Christopher Thomas Scott. "In its most mature form, ethics becomes policy—rules made by society to guide our best attempts to live a good life."[2]

In this chapter I show how the 14-day rule and related regulations for stem cell derivation are due to direct though unlabeled arguments that have arisen from within the embryo protection framework. In addition, the issue of payment or nonpayment to women who donate eggs is due in a more indirect way to discussions regarding justice taking place within the medical benefits framework.

Secular acceptance of the 14-day rule indicates that embryo protection is at work

One vivid example of unacknowledged theological influence on research ethics would be the increasing acceptance of the 14-day rule or an equivalent. Formulated more than two decades ago in the United Kingdom by philosopher Mary Warnock of the Warnock Committee,[3] the 14-day rule marks as an ethical threshold the adherence of the *in vivo* embryo to the mother's uterine wall and the appearance of the primitive streak. Prior to the fourteenth day, scientists should receive permission to carry on embryo research. This rule took hold in the U.K. and many other parts of the world, but not in United States guidelines for federal funding.

The National Academy of Sciences (NAS) in the United States studied the matter of stem cell research and, despite the precedent of federal funding policies, provided its own set of guidelines in 2005. Here we read that research should not be permitted that involves "*in vitro* culture of any intact human embryo, regardless of derivation method, for longer than 14 days or until formation of the primitive streak begins, whichever occurs first."[4] When the California Institute for Regenerative Medicine settled on its regulatory guidelines in 2006, it followed the NAS model. However, CIRM used the figure 12 instead of 14 days, just to play it safer.[5] Justification for such a rule is not provided by the NAS or CIRM documents themselves. The reader must presume the moral reasoning comes from elsewhere. No doubt it comes from the worldwide controversy and the contributions of the embryo protectionists.

Singapore makes the logic of secular embryo protection visible

The case of Singapore's Bioethics Advisory Commission (BAC) provides a clear example of the logic of embryo protection influencing public research guidelines. In June 2002 the BAC provided advisory guidelines which have since become *de facto* regulations for stem cell research at its giant facility, Biopolis. [6] Two items will be of interest here, reproductive cloning and rules for deriving new human embryonic stem cell lines.

When setting policy for reproductive cloning, Recommendation 7 of the BAC report said: "There should be a complete ban on the implantation of a human embryo created by the application of cloning technology into a womb, or any treatment of such a human embryo intended to result in its development into a viable infant." What seems clear is that Singapore, along with the rest of the world, offers no support for procreative cloning. This certainly agrees with the U.S. President's Council on Bioethics, which denounced reproductive cloning in the harsh words of its chair, Leon Kass. Kass's moral reasoning, recall, operated out of the nature protection framework.

When we turn to the derivation of new stem cell lines, the BAC carefully delineates a hierarchy of principles. The BAC approves the use of stem cells derived from adult tissues and also from cadaveric fetal tissues (human embryonic germ or hEG cells). With a tone of careful monitoring, the

BAC invokes beneficence as a moral guide, that is, the potential benefit to human health is a moral factor contributing to the approval of research. "Research involving the derivation and use of ES cells is permissible only where there is strong scientific merit in, and potential medical benefit from, such research." Then it proceeds to set a sequence of preferences for hES cell derivation; and this sequence obliquely reflects embryo protection reasoning. In Recommendation 4 we find: "Where permitted, ES cells should be drawn from sources in the following order: (1) existing ES cell lines, originating from ES cells derived from embryos less than 14 days old; and (2) surplus human embryos created for fertility treatment less than 14 days old." The first of these two reflects the restrictions of U.S. President George W. Bush's August 9, 2001, television address. The second reflects the discarded embryo position within the embryo protection framework.

After the options of using existing cell lines or activating a surplus embryo, might there be a third option, namely, the creation of fresh embryos for the purpose of research? Yes, but only after the first two options would be tried and found inadequate. Recommendation 5 puts it this way: "The creation of human embryos specifically for research can be justified only where (1) there is strong merit in, and potential medical benefit from, such research; (2) no acceptable alternative exists; and (3) on a highly selective, case-by-case basis, with specific approval from the proposed statutory body." As of

2006, no scientist had applied for permission to procure fresh embryos; so this provision has yet to be tried. Researchers to date obtain their embryonic material either from existing cell lines or the activation of frozen spare embryos obtained from IVF clinics.

Just what led to the Singapore Bioethics Advisory Committee's specific recommendations? First, in early 2002 the government of Singapore was responding to President Bush's previous speech in late summer 2001. On the one hand, Singapore wanted to woo scientists around the world to abandon their locations and come to Singapore's Biopolis to carry out their research. On the other hand, Singapore did not want to give the appearance of being lax on ethical standards. So, it created the BAC to study the matter, to come up with guidelines that would be respectable but not too restrictive.

En route to their June 2002 report, the BAC solicited theological input from the religious groups represented in this most pluralistic of societies: Hindus, Buddhists, Muslims, Orthodox Christians, Protestant Christians, and Roman Catholics. Of these groups, only the Protestants and Catholics put together teams of theologians and ethicists to think through the issues raised by genetic science in order to provide recommendations for public policy.[7] Leaders in the other religious traditions were appreciative that they would be consulted by the BAC; but they admitted they simply were not intellectually prepared to deal with such sophisticated scientific issues. When the BAC turned to make its own decisions, it emphasized that Singapore is a pluralistic society and that no single religious position could be permitted to dominate. What resulted in the BAC regulations could safely be called "secular."

What stands out clearly is the way in which the 14-day rule simultaneously provides a level of respect if not dignity to the early embryo while, at the same time, it grants permission to laboratory scientists to conduct experiments at the blastocyst stage.

Should we pay women who donate their eggs for stem cell research?

The Canadian Institutes of Health Research have set guidelines for research protocols.[8] We can see between the lines that consideration had to have been given to embryo protectionists. Yet, note what is emerging, namely, a concern for the women who donate eggs for scientific research. This is a justice concern. Justice concerns arise primarily from within the medical benefits framework. Let us take a closer look.

When it comes to public funding for work with human embryos, scientists taking public funds in Canada may work only under the following conditions:

- the embryos were created for reproductive purposes and are no longer required

- ⊚ cloning is prohibited
- ⊚ creating embryos solely for research purposes is prohibited
- the donors of the embryos have given free and informed consent
  - ⊚ consent must be renewed when embryos are actually used
- there were no commercial transactions involved in creating embryos
- research on stem cell lines created elsewhere will only be allowed if they were created in accordance with CIHR's guidelines
- research leading to human cloning would not be allowed
- combining non-human stem cells with a human embryo or fetus, or human stem cells with non-human embryos, is prohibited.

Note the exclusion of "commercial" means for obtaining embryonic research material. We can see emerging here another issue that has become an important item discussed from within the research standards framework, namely, the matter of paying women for egg donations.

When Proposition 71 was passed by California voters in 2004, the California Institute for Regenerative Medicine was prohibited from making financial payment to egg donors. Based on section 125290.35 b.3, the Science and Medical Standards Accountability Working Group was asked to set "standards prohibiting compensation to research donors or participants, while permitting reimbursement of expenses."[9] Now, we might ask: just what is going on here?

First, what is going on here with regard to the science? Observe that some aspects of laboratory research will require fresh eggs donated by women for the express use of experimentation. Curiously, if embryo derivation is restricted to discarded or spare zygotes that had been previously fertilized for purposes other than research, then we are not talking here about fresh zygotes. Or, are we?

Certainly research needs to proceed on the role of cytoplasm in gene expression and embryogenesis. And, for those pursuing nuclear transfer or so-called therapeutic cloning to establish histocompatibility, eggs to host the injected DNA nucleus will be required. This means laboratories will need women to step forward and offer their eggs. Should they be paid? Nearly all regulatory guidelines answer in the negative. Should they receive reimbursement for out-of-pocket expenses? Yes, is the answer given by CIRM. What is it that this kind of research needs? What is the gold standard for egg donation? First, the highest quality eggs come from younger women. Women between 21 and 35 move to the top of the list. Mothers of at least one biological child increase the promise of quality eggs. Second, eggs should be free from infectious viruses. Screening out excess genetic material becomes part of the selection process. Third, experience shows that clinics like to work with women willing to participate, who genuinely want to share what their bodies produce for the wider human welfare.

Second, what is going on here with regard to women? What does the procedure for egg retrieval mean for women considering donating eggs for stem cell research? In recent years plenty of women have offered themselves to clinics, willing to donate because they deem such research to be important. They voluntarily donate their eggs out of high-minded service. Making money is not the primary motive, experience is telling us. Making a contribution to cure Parkinson's or cancer is meaningful. At least this is what donating women to date have reported. We might think of them as unsung heroines.

However, retrieving unfertilized eggs from a woman's body is complicated and risky. Hormonal manipulation is necessary to stimulate production of as many eggs as possible. Normally, when nature governs a woman's cycles, eggs appear and disappear in sequence. When clinically stimulated, however, the woman hyperovulates and produces a large number of eggs all at once. A dozen eggs can be retrieved at the same time. This makes for efficiency, to be sure.

Yet there are health risks. Egg-donating women who later become pregnant might undergo ovarian hyperovulation syndrome. Such women could experience pain, manageable though annoying. Remaining eggs may become enlarged, sometimes by a factor of ten. Bleeding can occur in the short term. And the risk of ovarian cancer may go up in the long term. Any woman contemplating egg donation will need to assess all of these possibilities. Respect for the woman's autonomy—*voluntary and fully informed consent* among other things—is ethically required of the clinic and the researchers.

Ethicists do not want money to become an incentive. Nor do ethicists want to encourage trafficking in human bodily material for payment. Nevertheless, donating women could and should receive reimbursement for relevant expenses, travel, missed wages, and even child care.

Behind the brief statements we find in regulatory documents prescribing research standards lies a large concern for justice accorded to women in our society. "My concern is with justice," writes Suzanne Holland. She is concerned "that women—particularly poor women, women of color, and their children—are dealt a fair hand with respect to the uses and social costs of genetic technologies in general and stem cell technology in particular."[10]

Such justice concerns come to expression within the medical benefits framework in two forms, concerns over exploitation and concerns over access. Ethicists want to see regulatory structures put in place that will treat women donating eggs as persons with dignity, not merely as bodies that spit out research material. Financial incentives should avoid the Scylla of underpaying and thereby exploiting well-intentioned donors, and the Charybdis of overpaying and luring poorer women into new social inequities. Most importantly, the poor women among us as well as their families should eventually have access to the medical products that regenerative medicine promises. Knowing how expensive the initial investment is, plans must be put in place now to assure that the poorest of the poor will ultimately benefit by this powerful new set of medical therapies.

The Korean Scandal

In 2004 and 2005, Professor Hwang Woo Suk of Seoul National University in Korea made worldwide news for successfully employing nuclear transfer to establish histocompatible or patient-specific stem cell lines for nine individuals. Now we might ask: where did Dr. Hwang obtain his oocytes? Did he violate any ethical principles? Did he bribe or coerce them from his student assistants? Or did he pay women to donate them? Hwang publicly stated in May 2005 that all eggs had been harvested from volunteers without payment. By November of that year, this became disputed. The director of the Miz-Medi Hospital in Seoul, from which Hwang's lab obtained some of its oocytes, disclosed that each of the women had been paid the equivalent of U.S. $1400. South Korea's Health Ministry also disclosed that two junior scientists had given their own eggs for research. The latter was seen as particularly egregious. Critics describe a university laboratory as hierarchical; and in a society as influenced by the Confucian tradition as is South Korea, subordinates find themselves in a dependent relationship to their superiors. This dependency makes the situation *de facto* coercive. Had the Hwang research team exploited women to obtain their oocytes?

Dr. Hwang provoked additional criticisms as well. Independent investigations demonstrated that he had falsified evidence, that he failed to produce a single new stem cell line through nuclear transfer. Still worse, he was accused of embezzling grant funds, diverting them to his own private purposes. As of this writing, Dr. Hwang is facing a long and arduous court trial.[11]

What is significant for this discussion is that the world erupted with criticism that Dr. Hwang had violated tacit if not overt ethical codes by offering payment and even subtle coercion to the women who donated their eggs. What is at stake is the dignity and long-term health of women who might be willing to participate in stem cell research; and research standards are being set accordingly nearly everywhere.

Ronald M. Green, a Jewish scholar and former president of the Society for Christian Ethics, offers the moral reasoning that supports what seems to be increasingly adopted by research regulators. "Ovulation induction is an invasive medical procedure with known and undetermined risks. Not only must egg donors be informed of these risks, but steps also must be taken to preserve the voluntary nature of their consent. . . . It also includes avoiding undue financial incentives."[12]

Conclusion

The framework within which research ethics and regulations are worked out presupposes the medical benefits framework. As guidelines for the laboratory are formulated, we can see the influence of all three frameworks, especially the tidal influence of embryo protection. The stringent criteria for use of embryos in stem cell derivation as well as nearly universal adherence to the 14-day rule testify to this.

What is distinctive to the medical benefits framework that has come to influence research ethics is the low-key yet firm commitment to certain justice concerns. Commitment to the dignity and health of women belongs in this category. Suzanne Holland has laid down the rhetorical gauntlet that has been picked up by many regulatory drafting committees: "What is so compelling about moving forward with research on hES cells is the promise that it contains the potential for therapies that 'will serve to relieve human suffering,' as NBAC [the National Bioethics Advisory Committee during the Clinton administration] put it. But a feminist ethical analysis has to ask, whose suffering? and at whose expense?"[13]

7.

Theological Reflections on Human Nature

Theology is disciplined religious reflection. Perhaps one of the most urgent agenda items for the present generation of Christian theologians is development of a nuanced and compelling concept of the human person, usually termed a theological anthropology. The good news is that the public square welcomes theological input from Christian intellectuals, as it welcomes input from religious leaders in other traditions. What an otherwise pluralistic and secular society needs and wants is a coherent and inspiring doctrine of human nature that can provide grounding for making public policy. Might Christian theologians have something to contribute? Our present moment provides an opportunity, perhaps even a mandate.

Before jumping into the public square, I would like to return to distinctively Christian materials to construct a viable theological anthropology. In this chapter I plan to gather some foundational exegesis and theological reflection that pictures our human nature as determined more by our future than our past. Rather than appeal primarily to creation, I will appeal to new creation. Rather than appeal first to Adam and Eve, I will appeal first to the Easter Christ and our anticipated resurrection into eternal life with God. With this vision of our God-appointed future, I will ask if such an anticipatory anthropology can provide grounding and guidance for a transformatory ethical orientation.

Between the theological foundation and the ethical superstructure, I plan to build in a theory of human dignity. Because dignity plays such a decisive role in the stem cell ethical debate, it deserves a closer look. I will contend that dignity, rightly understood, is conferred before it is innate. To have dignity, one must be in relationship; a relationship confers dignity. One way to picture the Christian ethic of love is to see it as conferring dignity on persons who can then rise up to claim worth for themselves.

One of the implications of this theory is that a relational understanding of dignity undercuts the assumptions made by embryo protectionists, namely, that dignity is biologically based in an individual's genome. Dignity belongs to a relationship, ultimately a relationship to the future God has in store for us. It cannot be traced back to some point of origin, to the establishment of a new genetic code.

Should we ground our anthropology in archonic or epigenetic cosmology?

As we reflect on human nature from a biblical perspective, we should ask: where in the Bible should we go? Should we go back to the doctrine of creation, back to the story of Adam and Eve? Or, should we go to the other end of the Bible, to the apocalypse, to the vision of a transformed humanity experiencing abundant life in the new creation? Going backward is to think archonically. Going forward is to think epigenetically.

Let me explain what I mean. The term *archonic* calls to mind the ancient Greek word we find in the Bible, *arche*. This may be a little word, but its apron of meanings spreads widely. Note how *arche* appears in everyday speech in words such as: archaeology, monarchy, hierarchy, patriarchy, and such. This innocent little word *arche* combines two gigantic meanings. First, it means beginning or origin. Second, it means government or rule. Implicit is the principle that the way something begins governs its essence or identity. Whenever threatened by change or deterioration, archonic thinking seeks to return to the origin to retrieve essence.

The early chapters of Genesis fill a treasure chest of archisms. In the first eleven chapters we find one etiological narrative after another, each explaining the origin and hence the meaning of many contemporary experiences. Why is our week organized into seven days? Because God created the world in seven days; and our calendar week recalls this cosmic beginning. Why do we rest on the Sabbath? Because God rested on the first Sabbath. Why is the human race in such a mess? Because Adam and Eve ate the forbidden fruit and were expelled from the Garden. Why do the world's peoples speak different languages, and why do foreigners sound like they are babbling? Because at the Tower of Babel God confused our tongues when the human race, filled with *hubris* or pride, decided to build its own tower to heaven. The very title we have ascribed to this first book of Moses, Genesis, is an archonic word. It means onset or beginning or first creation.

Yet one might ask: does biblical thinking require that we answer all questions by going back to the beginning? Is the beginning definitive? Could new things also contribute to our reality? Was God done creating after the first seven days? Should we establish ethical principles that will take us back to some primordial essence; or should we construct ethics on a vision of something new drawing us toward the future?

Instead of Genesis, might we orient ourselves toward epigenesis? With the term *epi* on the front of *genesis*, we refer to a moment that marks a new beginning. What the future brings is a reality that surpasses the one we have inherited. Beyond creation we can anticipate new creation.

Does the Bible think epigenetically? Yes! "I am about to do a new thing," says God (Isa. 43:19). God might have rested on that first Sabbath, but

God is by no means done creating. The world we have inherited is not done yet. It is still on the way. God has much more to do yet.

God has yet to build the New Jerusalem and deliver it with a big red ribbon on it. The new City of God will bring to all of us and all of creation what Jesus' healing miracles anticipated. It is a vision beautifully evoked in the final and most misunderstood book of the Bible:

> Then I saw a new heaven and a new earth; for the first heaven and the first earth had passed away, and the sea was no more. And I saw the holy city, the new Jerusalem, coming down out of heaven from God, prepared as a bride adorned for her husband. And I heard a loud voice from the throne saying, "See, the home of God is among mortals. He will dwell with them; they will be his peoples, and God himself will be with them; he will wipe every tear from their eyes. Death will be no more; mourning and crying and pain will be no more, for the first things have passed away." (Rev. 21:1)

One fascinating feature of the coming New Jerusalem, I think, is what we find right downtown. "Then the angel showed me the river of the water of life, bright as crystal, flowing from the throne of God and of the Lamb through the middle of the street of the city. On either side of the river is the tree of life with its twelve kinds of fruit, producing its fruit each month; and the leaves of the tree are for the healing of the nations"

Rev. 22:1). Now, we might ask, just where did we bump into the river of life and the tree of life before? Well, we left them back in Genesis, in the Garden of Eden (Gen. 2:7-9). Here in the capitol of the new creation, the water of life and the tree of life are no longer restricted to a garden surrounded by wilderness. In the transformed future they bring life to the city, the center of metropolitan and perhaps even cosmic reality. The Book of Genesis did not have the last word. The story of creation did not end there. There is more to be told. It will culminate in new creation. On top of genesis we can anticipate epigenesis.

Rather than stick with past creation, we can quiz the Bible about future new creation. The drama of God's involvement in the history of Israel as well as the life of believers in Christ is the drama of redemption, of transformation. Christians live not only out of faith and love, but also out of hope. What we hope for is renewal, resurrection, and new life. Hope is one of the three theological virtues: "And now faith, hope, and love abide, these three; and the greatest of these is love" (1 Cor. 13:13). Even if hope takes a back seat to love, we cannot live the life of faith without it.

Hope keeps the eyes of faith future-oriented. So also does the life of beatitude, as articulated in Matthew 5:4: "Blessed are those who mourn, for they will be comforted." We might add: blessed are those who suffer now, for they will be healed. The New Testament word for salvation, *soteria* in Greek and *salvos* in Latin, literally means healing.

Healing and salvation stand before the eyes of faith as that for which we hope.

Can we think of human nature in terms of God's promised future?

As we turn from cosmology to anthropology, where do we orient our understanding of human nature? Do we orient it to our archonic past, on where we have come from? Was our essence determined at the beginning? Was the essence of the human race unchangeably fixed when God blew into the dust to create the first living human (Gen. 2:7)? Will the human race forever remain what it was during the first generation in evolutionary history when we grew a new branch on the family tree that we share with the primates? Should our ethics be oriented toward returning us to an archonic nature that allegedly existed before contaminated by scientific and technological modification?

Or, like the cosmos, is it the case that we are not done yet? Might it be the case that we are in for a transformation? Might it be the case that our essence is to be found in the future, not the past?

As I read the New Testament, it appears to me that the future takes precedence over the past, just as Christ takes precedence over Adam. The future can incorporate and include the past, but the past cannot incorporate or include the future. Grace takes precedence over sin, and transformation takes precedence over nature. To my reading, this is the flight that takes off when St. Paul compares

Christ and Adam in his Epistle to the Romans:

> Therefore just as one man's trespass led to condemnation for all, so one man's act of righteousness leads to justification and life for all. For just as by the one man's disobedience the many were made sinners, so by the one man's obedience the many will be made righteous. But law came in, with the result that the trespass multiplied; but where sin increased, grace abounded all the more, so that, just as sin exercised dominion in death, so grace might also exercise dominion through justification leading to eternal life through Jesus Christ our Lord. (Rom. 5:18-21)

Redemption trumps creation, or at least the fallen creation we today have inherited.

It seems to me that Karl Barth's interpretation launches us toward an illuminative re-grasping of the human situation. "Our unity with Adam is less essential and less significant than our true unity with Christ. . . . For Christ who seems to come second, really comes first, and Adam who seems to come first really comes second."[1] Barth's point is that with the advent of Jesus Christ, the human race is drawn up into a new definition of itself. What is astonishing, adds Wolfhart Pannenberg, is "Paul's reorientation of the concept of the human person as he turns away from the past and looks to the future of a new human being."[2]

I believe this connection between Christ and humanity is a central yet overlooked theme in

Christian anthropology. As Christians, we do not limit our self-definition to what we read about Adam and Eve. Oh yes, the Adam and Eve story brings to articulation some difficult-to-admit characteristics of human behavior. Like our first parents, we too find fruit on the tree of the knowledge of good and evil quite delectable. We eat, and we fall. On our way down we make excuses: "Blame them! Blame somebody else! Blame God, if you have to, but I'm innocent!" Our self-understanding as sinners who justify ourselves while blaming others could not find a more vivid portrayal than the Adam and Eve story.

But the Adam and Eve story is not the end of our story. Beyond sin and the blame game, we have been afforded the gift of forgiveness. Beyond the finality of death, we have been afforded the promise of new life. Christ is the pivot of history that marks the forthcoming change in our inherited human nature.

Our human essence—if one can speak of essence at all—is to be found not in our origin but in our destiny. And our destiny is pre-figured in Jesus Christ, in both his death and resurrection. We all die. Adam and Eve died. Jesus died. But Jesus also rose again on Easter. This Easter event was not merely a nice thing that happened to this otherwise badly treated boy from Nazareth. It was much more. Easter initiated a new chapter in cosmic history; and it introduced a new quality to the human reality. What happened to Jesus is destined to happen to us as well. "But in fact Christ has been raised from the dead, the first fruits of those who have died" (1 Cor. 15:20). What happened to Christ on Easter is scheduled to happen to us as well, at the advent of the new creation. To live now in hope is to include our future resurrection into our present understanding of ourselves.

Jesus rose with scars in his hands and his side, memories of his previous finite experience with human fallenness. Yet these scars were healed. Resurrection heals. It also transforms human existence as we have inherited it. To hope for the healing prophesied to arrive with the New Jerusalem is to live now with the expectation that full and complete healing will belong to who we understand ourselves to be. It is to live the life of beatitude.

Our essence or at least our identity as human persons or as a human race is not to be found at the beginning. Rather, it is to be found in our future. It is to be found in our destiny. Wolfhart Pannenberg relies on the double meaning of the German term *Bestimmung* to tease out this relationship. *Bestimmung* is frequently translated into English as "destiny." But, it could also be translated "determination."[3] Pannenberg's theological point is that our destiny determines our definition. Who we have always been is yet to be determined, determined by our destiny in the divine drama that is yet to reach its consummation in the new creation. "What a man will be is not already given by nature. He must first seek his destiny."[4]

Can we build relationality right into the definition of a human person?

This determining destiny is not an individualistic thing. Our promised resurrection is inextricably connected to the advent of the new creation. Our promised healing is dependent on the advent of healing for the entire community, perhaps even healing for the entire cosmos. "Only through anticipation of this future can human beings presently exist as themselves," writes Pannenberg. "Here, moreover, the identity of their present existence presupposes not only their personal future but also, in a way, the future of their people and their world and even the future of all humankind, since individuals are inseparable from their world."[5]

What Pannenberg shows is how we need to see that futurity and relationality come together in a single package. To understand our human existence rightly, we need to see ourselves today as existing in anticipation of a future relationship in which healing will have transformed both ourselves and our world.

I find that those theologians who stress the significance of relationality in establishing human identity to be putting us on the right track. Beginning with the trinitarian relations internal to the life of God, the late Catherine Mowry LaCugna grounded human relationality in divine relationality. "The ultimate ground and meaning of being is therefore communion among persons: God is ecstatic, fecund, self-emptying out of love for another, a personal God who comes to self through another. . . . The communion of divine life is God's communion *with us* in Christ and as Spirit."[6]

Marjorie Hewitt Suchocki also sees relationality both internal and external to the divine life; but her assertions are drawn less from trinitarian insights than they are from Whiteheadian process theology. Her relational theology "posits a dynamic union of all things with God in an interactive flow of time and everlastingness."[7] With this understanding of divine relationality, Suchocki can then ground an ethical vision of universal well-being. What she means by this is that our pursuit of the good should be the pursuit of the good for all, for the entire world, even for God. A local or parochial good does not suffice, because all things in reality are related to all other things. "To hold to a criterion of *universal* well-being, challenges every border we close, and ever raises before us the reality that in fact our interdependence is far wider than we can consciously know. Therefore, in spite of all the qualifications and difficulties, the impossible ideal of universal well-being is the most effective."[8]

If we begin with an understanding of God as relational, and if we add that our ultimate destiny as human beings is relational as well, how might this influence the way we formulate our ethical vision? Two features stand out. The first is the universal scope of our vision of well-being. The second is the future orientation that includes transformation, especially transformation understood as healing. Oh, yes, resurrection and consummate healing are transcendental concepts, to be sure; yet, we might ask whether they might inform our ethical framework for dealing with contemporary challenges, such as the stem cell controversy. At least one implication is clear: we ought not to advocate shutting down scientific or medical progress because we deem the pre-progressive past more sacred than the future. The healing that scientific medicine offers us could at minimum be placed in continuity with what we see as God's plan for healing the entire world. Science itself is not salvific, to be sure; but by relieving human suffering and enhancing human flowering, medical science fragmentarily incarnates ahead the grand healing that is God's eschatological promise.

Is dignity individual or relational?

One element of the stem cell controversy that comes up frequently, even if it is not analyzed frequently, is dignity. Within each of the three frameworks dignity plays the role of protector. In the embryo protection framework, opponents of stem cell research appeal to dignity to protect the embryo from destruction. In the nature protection framework, dignity is loosely tied to our inherited human nature; and this becomes the warrant for repelling genetic science and technology. In the medical benefits framework, the appeal to beneficence includes the assumption that persons who suffer from serious diseases and injuries have dignity; they have worth. Perhaps it might be worthwhile analyzing the concept of dignity in light of some of the anthropological considerations mentioned above.

We in the post-Enlightenment period assume that the concept of dignity refers us to the intrinsic value of an individual human person.[9] The value of a person cannot be reduced to his or her instrumental worth. This implies that we are always worth more than our possessions or our reputations or our function in the economy. As persons with dignity, we ought not be reduced to the subjective value of those who like or dislike us. We are confident we can claim our rights even when everyone around dislikes us. Dignity applies to individual persons. And as individual persons we are always an end and never merely a means to some other greater value. It is this dimension of intrinsic value that constitutes human dignity as we know it in the modern West.

Now let us ask a phenomenological question: is dignity intrinsic or conferred? It is both. When young children grow up in a family in which they receive love, they grow in self-worth. When their parents treat them as valuable, they begin to see themselves as valuable. Eventually, they claim that value for themselves. Phenomenally, dignity is first conferred, then claimed.

Theologically, we believe our human dignity is ultimately conferred by God. Furthermore, because we have experienced God treating us with dignity, we now confer it on one another. Once we have conferred dignity on someone we love, we treat that person as having intrinsic value. This is the nature of love, namely, to treat the beloved as an end and not a means to some further end.

A few years ago I wrote a book on the role genetics might play in family planning, *For the Love of Children*. In it I included a theological maxim: *God loves each of us regardless of our genetic make-up, and we should do likewise.* This was my geneticized adaptation of 1 John 4:11: "Beloved, since God loved us so much, we also ought to love one another."[10]

One of the ways that we have learned about God's conferral of dignity on us is through the ministry of the incarnate Son. Jesus' ministry took him to the most humble of persons in first-century Israel: the beggars, the lepers, those crippled or blind from birth, and to such social outcasts as adulterers or traitorous tax collectors. Jesus took a special interest in those among us who suffer marginalization, or who just plain suffer. Jesus was particularly concerned about children. "Let the little children come to me, and do not stop them," he said, "for it is to such as these that the kingdom of heaven belongs" (Matt. 19:14). Conferring dignity was an ethical activity for Jesus and, correspondingly, is for us.

One might describe the ethical mandate to love our neighbor as a mandate to confer dignity, especially on persons who do not yet claim that dignity. Children belong in this category. Might we think of the poor and oppressed in this world as persons lacking in respectful treatment? We know that the outcasts are loved by God, so, in this sense, that dignity transcends anything we do. Yet the act of conferring dignity emboldens a person to rise up and claim the sense of worth.

All human persons are loved by God regardless of their lot in life or how others have treated them. If God loves them, so should all of society. Our society should exemplify this divine love in at least a minimal way through enforcing laws that show respect and honor to each individual, regardless of social station. Karen Lebacqz has pressed this concern forward in her writings as the pursuit of justice.[11]

No, dignity is not biological! It is relational!

It is almost a contemporary truism to say what theologian and expert on robotics Anne Foerst says, "Every form of personhood is based on the acceptance of the other as the other."[12] This is a relational picture of personhood. What, then, can we say about the belief that personhood understood as dignity is innate, inborn, inherent in nature? What can we say about the embryo protectionist position that associates dignity not with relationship but with genetic uniqueness at conception? What can we say about those who want to anchor dignity in the individual biology of the zygote?

Renee Mirkes articulates both the contemporary Roman Catholic position and the eighteenth-century

Enlightenment position on innate dignity while opposing what he dubs the "social contract theory of personhood." He argues that "Human personhood inheres in the human being naturally. Therefore, the role of an extraneous moral agent is to discover human personhood in someone based on the individual's humanhood, not to arbitrarily construct and award it to another."[13] Now, how should we react? On the one hand, I want to say, "Yes, indeed." We affirm that dignity is inherent, almost by definition. On the other hand, can we find that dignity located in our biology? Does dignity register with our genome? No, one would search in vain to find dignity in the genes. We treat persons as if they were born with dignity because God treats all persons this way; and we wish to treat all persons as God does. Actual dignity is found in this relational conferring, not in the DNA. The conceptus in the petri dish, outside the mother's body, is not in a dignity-conferring relationship.

The value and significance of dignity understood as inherent for our legal system is obvious. Such a dignity doctrine permits us in court to defend the rights of every individual regardless of how humble he or she might be. Every person has a right to *dignitas* before the law. We don't want to surrender this.

But to derive dignity from our biology at conception is a mistake, in my judgment. Dignity—at least the sense of dignity understood as self-worth— is not simply genetic. Rather, it is the fruit of a relationship, an ongoing loving relationship.

This seems to be obviously the case. A newborn welcomed into the world by a mother and father who provide attention and affection develops a self-consciousness that incorporates this attention and affection as evidence of self-worth. As consciousness becomes constituted, this sense of worth can be claimed for oneself, and individual dignity develops. We are first treated with dignity, then we claim it for ourselves.

It is my judgment that genetic uniqueness simply cannot count as a measure of personhood, dignity, or moral protectability. As we have seen, naturally occurring monozygotic twins share identical genomes and possible future cloned persons would as well; and it would be absurd to deny such persons their personhood or dignity. Yet genetic uniqueness seems attractive to some ethicists; and ethicists clamor to impart some special moral status to it. But I fear this attraction is due to the legacy of effete individualism; and in their haste such ethicists risk supporting an unrealistic view of individual autonomy.

Nature is more relational. Even DNA does not make a person a person all by itself. To the point here is my earlier observation that once the embryo attaches to the mother's uterine wall about the fourteenth day, it receives hormonal signals from the mother that precipitate the very gene expression necessary for growth and development into a child. *Time* magazine once offered a cover story, "Inside the Womb," that illustrates the importance of this observation. The child's "genes engage the environment of the womb in an elaborate conversation, a two-way dialogue that involves not only the air its mother breathes and the water she drinks but also what drugs she takes, what diseases she contracts and what hardships she suffers."[14] Biological uniqueness does not imply independence; we are who we are because of our relationships.

The genomic dignity position has embraced its own version of the Enlightenment stress on the autonomous individual. On the one hand, individual autonomy is an important value, but only when applied appropriately. On the other hand, it fails to recognize that no early embryo can become an individual unless its genes are prompted to express themselves by the triggering hormones of the mother. To be a person is to be a person-in-relationship. An early embryo *ex vivo*, outside a mother's body, cannot become a person in the biological sense, let alone an autonomous individual. Where this leads is this: morally protectable dignity could justifiably apply to an early embryo *in vivo*, in the mother's body; but it should not apply *ex vivo*, in the laboratory petri dish.

Conclusion

Now, after trumpeting all these assertions about our relational future and the need to see dignity as first conferred before claimed as innate, I would like to offer the decisive insight into the public policy debate. I would like to resolve to everyone's satisfaction the unnerving tension over the moral status of the early embryo. I would like to offer a theory of human dignity that would decide the issue without any lingering ambiguity.

But, alas, my theological reflections and ethical constructions fall short. When the question is formulated—what is the moment of ensoulment and the establishment of morally protectable dignity?—I must confess, I cannot on the basis of my reflections provide a definitive answer. I am confident that what I have said about human dignity is on target; but it does not lend itself to answering precisely this question.

I could imagine saying that once the mother has a relationship with the embryo attached to her uterine wall, her care becomes the way she confers dignity on the unborn. Social support for such mothers becomes the way our society confers such dignity. Yet what I fail to provide is the criterion by which to measure whether the *ex vivo* blastocyst contains some individual quality that requires us to confer dignity on it. When this is the question, I hesitate to proffer an apodictic answer.

Yet I am willing to tender a cautious answer. My cautious answer is based upon the observation that the *ex vivo* blastocyst does not exist in relationship to a mother; and, therefore, it really has no potential to become a human person. Without this relationship, talk of potential based upon a unique genetic codes is meaningless. Therefore, here is my considered judgment: no, the blastocyst outside the mother's body possesses no innate quality of human dignity. It does not stand up on its own and demand that we treat it with moral protectability. Those who do stand up and provide us with an opportunity to love and to impute dignity are suffering people, those whose lives could come to fuller flower with regenerative therapy. Supporting regenerative medicine confers dignity on living persons and future persons who are victimized by suffering.

Perhaps the reason I cannot definitively answer the embryo protection question has to do with the way the question is formulated. Nevertheless, I do not want to pass the buck. I recognize the integrity of the Vatican when formulating this and related commitments based upon the assumptions of Roman Catholic anthropology. Yet, as it turns out, my own reflections lead toward a non-compossible alternative.

Still, I stand by what I have enunciated. Rather than something imparted with our genetic code or accompanying us when we are born, dignity is the future end result of God's saving activity, which we anticipate socially when we confer dignity on those who do not yet claim it. The ethics of God's kingdom in our time and in our place consists of conferring dignity and inviting persons to claim dignity as a prolepsis of its future fulfillment.

The biblical mandate to love one another means, among other things, imputing dignity to all persons in such a way that they may rise up and claim self-worth for themselves and share in the benefits of living together on this planet. So our contemporary ethical mandate is similar: we should confer dignity on human persons so that they may rise up to claim dignity for themselves.

8.

Can Theological Ethicists
Help Anybody?

Here is the question I would like to address in this final chapter: which is better, to be right or to help somebody? Or, to put it more concretely, what is the task of the theologically informed ethicist: to get it right or to aid people who need to make concrete decisions?

The choice between apodictic rightness or cautious judgments

When describing the confusion in the public square due to the smoke of ethical guns going off, firing at other ethicists, I earlier cited Ann Kiessling and Scott Anderson. "There are simply too many diametrically opposed theologies—many claiming to be the actual word of God—to reach a consensus."[1] Ronald Reagan Jr., who is the son of the late Alzheimer's-afflicted president and who is impatient with the U.S. government's slowness to invest in regenerative medicine, has fired his own shot. "It does not follow that the theology of a few should be allowed to forestall the health and well-being of the many."[2]

From the perspective of a bystander, watching the moral shootout, one might think that theological ethicists should be embarrassed. What gets heard is obstructionism, parochialism, atavism, absolutism. What gets portrayed is that ethicists, short on scientific knowledge, start firing their moral machine guns before they have determined just who might be their friends or enemies. All that counts, so it appears, is that ethicists are sufficiently pumped up with their own self-righteousness that they are willing to become heroes in the cause of what is right.

What might be the path to peace? Let's test one idea that goes like this: ask the theological ethicists to give up their absolutism. Ask them to deny that they speak the actual Word of God and acknowledge that they are voicing their own perspectives or opinions. Margaret Farley seems to concur with such a diagnosis and prescription: "Both sides claim a certain amount of epistemic humility, since there are only degrees of certainty available regarding the ontological status of the early embryo."[3] Rather than rendering absolute judgments, epistemic humility would suggest that we agree to degrees of certainty and withdraw from a cocksure attitude about what is right.

Is this what Kiessling and Anderson are asking of theological ethicists, epistemic humility? The assumption seems to be that strong convictions make for difficult moral deliberation. Weaker convictions, in contrast, would keep the ethical discussion civil and manageable.

The assumption here is that no one would voluntarily go to the lions defending a mere perspective or opinion. No one would sacrifice for epistemic humility. So a tentative person would become much less obnoxious in the public debate. What we need are ethicists who are less apodictic and more cautious. This will make them less courageous and more accommodating. In the public square the smoke would dissipate and . . . and then what?

Do ethicists sin?

Is this an adequate analysis? No, I do not think so. It is helpful, but not adequate.

Outside Christian anthropology, it may look like the fundamental human problem is absolutism. The problem with absolutism, so it appears, is that it leads to intolerance. Allegedly, repudiation of absolutism leads to tolerance, peace, and cooperation. But beware. To believe that repudiation of absolutism could do all this is to believe that the next telemarketing phone call will make one rich.

Despite the naïveté here, the logic appears on the surface to make sense. If ethical absolutism is the problem, then it would follow that we need to combat absolutism with recognition of our finitude, recognition of the perspectival and partial quality of our moral judgments. However, this fails as a diagnosis and prescription, because it is gnostic. As gnostic, it presumes that the human problem is ignorance, and that absolutism is a form of disguised ignorance. Education is always the remedy for ignorance. Those who are truly educated can provide salvation, according to gnostic logic; because they are aware of the finitude of their own judgments.

Socrates was gnostic in his conviction that knowledge would solve human problems. His *gnosis* contained an element of agnosticism, however, because he confessed that there were things he did not know and needed to learn. He claimed to be the most knowledgeable person in ancient Athens because he, and he alone, knew that he had limitations. Socrates recognized he had limitations that more prideful and hence more foolish people would refuse to admit to. Knowledge of his lack of knowledge was Socrates's saving knowledge.

In our situation, theological ethicists could benefit themselves and the rest or us if they would learn that they know less than they think they know. Our previous criticism of theological ethicists for pomposity in advocating uncompromising and apodictic moral claims would seem to provide an adequate diagnosis.

This diagnosis is helpful, but incomplete. Christian anthropology adds a relevant insight here. The Christian insight suggests that the problem is not simply absolutism, nor is the solution education about our limits. Rather, the deeper problem is self-justification. Every human being wants to find himself or herself in the right, as the Adam and Eve story testifies. So passionate are we to find ourselves in the right that we would blame anybody and everybody else as mistaken or even evil, if it would help make the case that we are right. It is part of the character of human fallenness that we claim righteousness for ourselves, even if to do so we must deny it to others. It is a human trait to draw the line between good and evil and place ourselves on the good side. In order to judge ourselves as good, we will place anybody and everybody, including God, on the evil side. This is human nature as we have inherited it.

Now, here is the kicker. Among the human population, the greatest sinners are the ethicists. Ethicists work professionally at drawing the line between good and evil and the result, conveniently, is that they routinely if not always find themselves on the good side. Because the general human propensity for self-justification is so intense, it infects the judgment of ethicists too. And because ethicists are so sophisticated, their arguments for their own self-justification are much more impenetrable than those the average person raises. Perhaps this is why onlookers to the public moral debate find themselves so frustrated with know-it-all ethicists.

Now, let me be clear. It belongs to the universal human condition that we seek to justify ourselves; we all draw the line between good and evil and place ourselves on the good side of the line. Ethicists represent an intensification and a sophistication of this general human propensity. It is not my intent to blame ethicists here. Firing at ethicists would only contribute to the problem, not help us see a way through it.

The theological word for what we are talking about is *sin*. Ethicists, whether they like it or not, fit the category of sin more squarely than warmongers and genocide perpetrators. As hard as this grapefruit-sized insight is to swallow, it is what we have learned about human nature from both the Adam and Eve story as well as the crucifixion story. Good people who justify themselves crucify. Ethicists crucify. When the smoke clears in the public square, the bodies of those shot down by ethical invectives become visible.

With this diagnosis, what is the prescription? It is repentance. Ethicists need to repent. They need to turn from the temptation to justify their positions in absolutist and final and dogmatic form. They need to repent from the desire to see themselves or their church or their ideology as absolutely right.

Having said this, I must grant that some value is to be found in the gnostic diagnosis on the difficulty posed by apodictic claims. Still, the problem to be dealt with is the ethicist's desire to place himself or herself on the good side of the line. The problem to be dealt with is to move the agenda away from the justification of the ethicist and toward the love the ethicist could show to those in the public square who might need love.

Note that I am not rejecting the gnostic insight. Yes, there is a problem when ethicists speak as though their finite judgments contain eternal and absolute authority. Yes, there is a problem when flawed reasoning parades as eternal truth. But what I believe we need to add is attention to the focal subject of the ethicist's judgments. Is the task of the ethicist to render *obiter dicta* that get it right? Or is the task of the ethicist to aid persons and organizations to make decisions amidst an array of confusing and difficult-to-understand choices? Is the focal task to support the doctrine or ideology or institution he or she represents? Or is the task to provide useful and helpful moral reasoning that others might benefit from? Such other-directedness is the only hope of saving an ethicist's soul, so to speak.

One of the features of life in our modern and emerging postmodern world replete with exploding globalization is the bombardment of a seemingly infinite array of choices. Increased choice is the hallmark of globalized consciousness. New discoveries in science increase the range of data we need to incorporate to understand the human condition and even to understand ourselves. New developments in technologies, especially genetic technologies, present a nearly unfathomable array of opportunities. As the existentialist philosopher Jean-Paul Sarte would frequently say, we are condemned to freedom. We are free to choose, while we are not free not to choose. Unless an ethicist can help us through the process of making choices in this new situation, we will find the field of ethics unhelpful.

Can ethicists help us make decisions?

What our people need and what our society needs is good solid moral reasoning that does not appear to be so ideologically dependent that it is uncompromising. Rather, such moral reasoning needs to illumine our path and show directions that decision-making might take us. Can the ethicist provide the kind of moral reasoning that will help people other than themselves make decisions?

Let me provide an example to ponder, namely, Ronald Green. Green has been a *pro bono* consultant to Michael D. West at Advanced Cell Technology in Boston. In fact, he has been chairing the Ethics Advisory Board at ACT. Green argues this way: "hES cell and therapeutic cloning research is both therapeutically important and ethically acceptable. In my view, the moral claims of the very early embryo do not outweigh those of children and adults that can be helped by hES cell and therapeutic cloning technologies."[4]

Let me point out three things. First, Green seems to play into the public confusion by assuming a competition between the dignity of the blastocyst and the dignity of those who could benefit from regenerative medicine. As I said earlier, this is confusing because no competition between these two exists within any single ethical framework. The confusion in the public debate is due to multiple non-compossible ethical frameworks.

Second, by using the phrase, "in my view," Green has disavowed apodictic or dogmatic status for his moral judgment. He is not an absolutist. He is a perspectivalist. He would pass the gnostic test, according to which we recognize the limits of our perspective.

Third, Green is providing advice and counsel to society regarding how to proceed on stem cell research. He is implicitly acknowledging that we find ourselves in a new and complex situation—this is the first time a society has had to wrestle with the stem cell issue. He has studied the matter. He has arrived at his own judgment. Now, he wants to pass on to the rest of society the fruits of his ethical labors. He is laying before the rest of us the opportunity to make public policy decisions that will incorporate, among other things, his moral reasoning. What I like about this, is that Green offers his best moral judgment—his "view"—in such as way that decision makers can draw it into their decision-making. This is a commendable model.

Decisions, decisions, decisions

When we consider the array of new genetic technologies associated with bringing children into the world—IVF with donors or IVF with genetic selection, preimplantation genetic diagnosis combined with genetic selection, *in vivo* genetic analysis, and on the horizon genetic enhancement and perhaps even germline intervention—we can imagine the temporary confusion that parents-to-be must go through in making decisions. Families have more choices than McDonald's has hamburgers. How should they go about making decisions in light of these choices?

Not only families find themselves confronted with a baffling menu of options. So does our larger society. The options surrounding supporting or not supporting regenerative medical research are but one set. And, recognizing the speed and complexity of scientific research and technological innovation, we can safely forecast that the array of choices will only increase over the next half-decade and for the foreseeable future. This is the situation within which the human race finds itself.

One of the difficulties with embryo protectionists and nature protectionists is that they wish they were living in a different world. They wish they were living in a bygone world where new knowledge would not upset previously held assumptions about human nature, and where technology would be too weak to change anything essential. They believe they have an anchor in how human life should rightly be lived; and they are disturbed by the tossing sea whipped up by these new developments. What they perceive to be the responsibility of the ethicist is to say a loud no, to damn up the flow, to stop the train, to bring the plane back down onto the runway, to halt the advance. And if science and society continue to fly off in these allegedly dangerous directions, at least the ethicist can be comforted in knowing he or she was right all along.

Now I might be slightly overstating the case here, because both the embryo protectionists and nature protectionists I work with have a caring disposition toward those they wish to protect. Yet I wish to point out that these positions do not go far enough to be helpful to our society in the present situation. What we as a people need is solid and lucid moral reasoning that provides guidance in decision-making, not only for today but for facing new and foreseen developments that will confront us tomorrow. Being abstractly right is nice; but being concretely helpful is better, I think.

In addition, I believe we need a firm but flexible form of ethical deliberation that constructs counsel based upon a positive vision of the human future, not a wistful desire to return to our biological past. A biblical theology reports God's promises that the future will be better than the past. Redemption and salvation belong to the gospel vision of what we human beings can ultimately become. Transformation will be our destiny.

The divine promise of eschatological transformation is well beyond our control. This ultimate newness can be wrought only by the power and grace of God. Yet Scripture's salvific promise is a clue to how we should understand our lives. If God plans to bring big changes in the future, then it would not be unethical for us to plan to bring modest changes within our temporal realm. And because God's ultimate transformation will include the healing of all ills, an ethic that focuses on whatever healing science and technology can muster now has an undeniable affinity with what God has in store for us. To point out paths of moral guidance based upon a vision of a better human future would befit an ethical framework built on this kind of theological groundwork.

Notes

1. The Science of Stem Cells

1. Robert Lanza, ed., *Handbook of Stem Cells*, 2 vols. (Amsterdam: Elsevier Academic Press, 2004), 1:xxv.

2. Catherine M. Verfaillie, "Adult Stem Cells: Tissue Specific or Not?" in ibid., 2:14.

3. Douglas A. Melton and James W. Wilson, "Stemness: Definitions, Criteria and Standards," in ibid., 2:xxiii.

4. Actually, the procedure gaining attention would involve removal of a single blastomere from an early embryo during preimplantation genetic diagnosis. Then the remaining blastomeres would be implanted in the woman's body and a pregnancy is expected to result. Joe Leigh Simpson, "Blastomeres and Stem Cells," *Nature* 444:7118 (23 November 2006): 432-35.

5. Ariff Bongso, Chui-Yee Fong, Soon-Chye Ng, and Shan Ratnam, "Isolation and Culture of Inner Cell Mass Cells from Human Blastocysts," *Human Reproduction* 9:11 (1994): 2110-17.

6. James A. Thomson, Joseph Itskovitz-Eldor, Sander S. Shapiro, Michelle A. Waknitz, Jennifer J. Swiergiel, Vivienne S. Marshall, and Jeffrey M.

Jones, "Embryonic Stem Cell Lines Derived from Human Blastocysts," *Science* 282 (6 November 1998): 1145-47.

7. Both patents, 5,843,780 (1998) and 6,200,806 (2001) have the same name: "Primate Embryonic Stem Cells." Note that we human beings are here referred to as primates.

8. Michael J. Shamblott, Joyce Axelman, Shunping Wang, Elizabeth M. Bugg, John W. Littlefield, Peter J. Donovan, Paul D. Blumenthal, George R. Huggins, and John D. Gearhart, "Derivation of Pluripotent Stem Cells from Cultured Human Primordial Germ Cells," *Proceedings of the National Academy of Sciences* 95 (November 1998): 13726-31.

9. Thomas B. Okarma, "Human Embryonic Stem Cells: A Primer on the Technology and Its Medical Applications," *The Human Embryonic Stem Cell Debate: Science, Ethics, and Public Policy*, ed. Suzanne Holland, Karen Lebacqz, and Laurie Zoloth (Cambridge and London: MIT Press, 2001), 3.

2. Framing the Public Discussion of Stem Cell Ethics

1. Laurie Zoloth, "Immortal Cells, Moral Selves," *Handbook of Stem Cells*, ed. Robert Lanza, 2 vols. (Amsterdam: Elsevier Academic Press, 2004), 1:747.

2. Robert Benne, *The Paradoxical Vision: A Public Theology for the Twenty-First Century* (Minneapolis: Fortress Press, 1995), 222.

3. Lisa Sowle Cahill, book review of *The Human Embryonic Stem Cell Debate* in *National Catholic Bioethics Quarterly* 2:3 (Autumn 2002): 559-62.

4. Ann A. Kiessling and Scott Anderson, *Human Embryonic Stem Cells* (Boston: Jones and Bartlett Publishers, 2003), 197.

5. Ibid.

3. The Embryo Protection Framework

1. The National Council of the Churches of Christ in the USA, "Fearfully and Wonderfully Made: A Policy on Human Biotechnologies," http://www.ncccusa.org/pdfs/BioTechPolicy.pdf, lines 307-308.

2. A fuller exposition of this as well as the other frameworks will appear in a book I am currently preparing with two co-authors, Karen Lebacqz and Gaymon Bennett, tentatively titled, *Immortal Lines: Theologians Say "Yes" to Stem Cells.*

3. Center for Bioethics and Culture Network (CBC): www.thecbc.org. "First Do No Harm": www.donoharm.org.uk/.

4. Congregation for the Doctrine of the Faith, "Instruction on Respect for Human Life in Its Origins and on the Dignity of Procreation," (*Donum Vitae*) (22 February 1987), *Acta Apostolicae Sedis* 1988 (80), 70-102. See also: John Paul II, *Evangelium Vitae* (25 March 1995), *Acta Apostolicae Sedis* 1995, (87), 401-522.

5. Pope John Paul II, *The Gospel of Life* (New York: Random House, Times Books, 1995).

6. John Breck, *The Sacred Gift of Life: Orthodox Christianity and Bioethics* (Crestwood, N.Y.: St. Vladimir's Seminary Press, 1998), 259.

7. Nigel M. de S. Cameron, *The New Medicine: Life and Death after Hippocrates* (Chicago and London: Bioethics Press, 1991, 2001), 100-101.

8. Gilbert Meilaender, "Some Protestant Reflections," *The Human Embryonic Stem Cell Debate: Science, Ethics, and Public Policy*, ed. Suzanne Holland, Karen Lebacqz, and Laurie Zoloth (Cambridge and London: MIT Press, 2001), 142.

9. Southern Baptist Convention, "Resolution: On Human Embryonic and Stem Cell Research," cited in *God and the Embryo*, ed. Brent Waters and Ronald Cole-Turner (Washington, D.C.: Georgetown University Press, 2003), 180.

10. Hippocrates, *Epidemics*, 1:xi in W.H.S. Jones, *Hippocrates with an English Translation* (Cambridge, Mass.: Harvard University Press, 1959), 1:165.

11. Gene Outka, "The Ethics of Human Stem Cell Research," *God and the Embryo*, 31.

12. Frist's speech quoted by Michael Bellomo, *The Stem Cell Divide* (New York: American Management Association, 2006), 100.

13. Richard Doerflinger, "The Policy and Politics of Embryonic Stem Cell Research," *National Catholic Bioethics Quarterly* 1:2 (Summer 2001): 143.

14. H. Tristram Engelhardt, Jr., *The Foundations of Christian Bioethics* (Lisse: Swets and Zeitlinger, 2000), 261.

15. "Embryonic Stem Cell Research in the Perspective of Orthodox Christianity: A Statement of the Holy Synod of Bishops of the Orthodox Church in America," cited in *God and the Embryo*, 173.

16. Pontifical Academy for Life, "Declaration on the Production and the Scientific and Therapeutic Use of Human Embryonic Stem Cells," cited in *God and the Embryo*, 167.

17. Catherine M. Verfaillie, "Adult Stem Cells: Tissue Specific or Not?" *Handbook of Stem Cells*, ed. Robert Lanza, 2 vols. (Amsterdam: Elsevier Academic Press, 2004), 2:14.

18. Norman Ford, *The Prenatal Person: Ethics from Conception to Birth* (Oxford: Blackwell, 2002), 160, Ford's italics. See also Margaret A. Farley, "Stem Cell Research: Religious Considerations," *Handbook of Stem Cells*, 770.

19. Ann A. Kiessling and Scott Anderson, *Human Embryonic Stem Cells* (Boston: Jones and Bartlett Publishers, 2003), 194.

20. Karen Lebacqz, "On the Elusive Nature of Respect," *The Human Embryonic Stem Cell Debate*, 159.

21. Thomas A. Shannon, "Grounding Human Dignity," *Dialog*, 43:2 (Summer 2004): 117.

22. Meilaender, "Some Protestant Reflections," 145.

23. Lisa Sowle Cahill, "Stem Cells: A Bioethical Balancing Act," *America*, 184:10 (2001), 14-19.

4. The Nature Protection Framework

1. Philip Hefner, "The Genetic 'Fix': Challenge to Christian Faith and Community," *Genetic Testing and Screening*, ed. Roger A. Willer (Minneapolis: Kirk House, 1998), 76.

2. See: President's Council on Bioethics, *Monitoring Stem Cell Research* (2004) and *Beyond Therapy: Biotechnology and the Pursuit of Happiness* (2004) located online at: http://www.bioethics.gov.

3. Leon R. Kass, *Life, Liberty and the Defense of Dignity: The Challenge for Bioethics* (San Francisco: Encounter Books, 2002), 146.

4. Ibid., 167.

5. Leon R. Kass and James Q. Wilson, *The Ethics of Human Cloning* (Washington, D.C.: AEI Press, 1998), 18.

6. See: Ted Peters, *Playing God? Genetic Determinism and Human Freedom*, 2d ed. (New York and London: Routledge, 2002), for an extensive analysis of the Promethean myth at work in modern society.

7. Kass and Wilson, *The Ethics of Human Cloning*, 18.

8. Jeremy Rifkin, *Algeny* (New York: Viking, 1983), 252.

9. Zoloth, "Immortal Cells, Moral Selves," *Handbook of Stem Cells*, ed. Robert Lanza, 2 vols. (Amsterdam: Elsevier Academic Press, 2004), 1:749.

10. "Embryonic Stem Cell Research in the Perspective of Orthodox Christianity: A Statement

of the Holy Synod of Bishops of the Orthodox Church in America," cited in *God and the Embryo*, ed. Brent Walters and Ronald Cole-Turner (Washington, D.C.: Georgetown University Press, 2003), 174.

11. Charles Krauthammer, Personal Statement in *Human Cloning and Human Dignity: The Report of the President's Council on Bioethics* (New York: Public Affairs, 2002), 328.

12. Christopher Thomas Scott, *Stem Cell Now* (New York: Pi Press, 2006), 187.

13. Ann A. Kiessling and Scott Anderson, *Human Embryonic Stem Cells* (Boston: Jones and Bartlett Publishers, 2003), 196.

14. Stanley Shostak, *Becoming Immortal: Combining Cloning and Stem Cell Therapy* (Albany, N.Y.: SUNY Press, 2002), 43.

15. Michael D. West, *The Immortal Cell* (New York: Doubleday, 2003), 212.

16. Ibid., 226, West's italics.

5. The Medical Benefits Framework

1. "The California Stem Cell Research and Cures Initiative" of 2004. Text of Proposition 71 at: http://www.cirm.ca.gov/prop71/pdf/prop71.pdf.

2. See articles by Ted Peters and Gaymon Bennett, Jr.: "Cloning in the White House," *Dialog* 41:3 (Fall 2002): 241-44; "Defining Human Life: Cloning, Embryos, and the Origins of Dignity," *Beyond Determinism and Reductionism: Genetic Science and the Person*, ed. Mark L.Y. Chan and Roland Chia (Adelaide, Australia: ATF Press, 2003), 56-73; "A Plea for Beneficence: Reframing the Embryo Debate," *God and the Embryo*, ed. Brent Walters and Ronald Cole-Turner (Washington, D.C.: Georgetown University Press, 2003), 111-30.

3. "Cloning Research, Jewish Tradition and Public Policy: A Joint Statement by the Union of Orthodox Jewish Congregations of America and the Rabbinical Council of America," cited in *God and the Embryo*, 204.

4. Elliot N. Dorff, *Matters of Life and Death: A Jewish Approach to Modern Medical Ethics* (Philadelphia and Jerusalem: Jewish Publication Society, 1998), 15.

5. Ibid., 26.

6. Jewish voices have been heard in support of stem cell research. Jewish theology emphasizes the divine mandate to steward medical science in the service of human welfare, and this applies positively to stem cell research. See: http://www.ou.org/public/statements/2001/nate34.htm and http://uahc.org/cgi-bin/resodisp.pl?file=fetaltissue&year=1993o.

7. Elliott N. Dorff, "Stem Cell Research–A Jewish Perspective," *The Human Embryonic Stem Cell Debate: Science, Ethics, and Public Policy*, ed. Suzanne Holland, Karen Lebacqz, and Laurie Zoloth (Cambridge and London: MIT Press, 2001), 92.

8. Laurie Zoloth, "Immortal Cells, Moral Selves," *Handbook of Stem Cells*, ed. Robert Lanza, 2 vols. (Amsterdam: Elsevier Academic Press, 2004), 2:753.

9. Moshe David Tendler, "Stem Cell Research and Therapy: A Judeo-Biblical Perspective, Ethical Issues in Human Stem Cell Research," in *Religious Perspectives* (September 1999), at NBAC Web site: http://bioethics.gov/pubs.html.

10. For an ethic that begins with a vision of a redeemed future and applies it to scientific and technological progress, see Ted Peters, *Anticipating Omega* (Göettingen: Vandenhoeck & Ruprecht, 2006).

11. Margaret A. Farley, "Stem Cell Research: Religious Considerations," *Handbook of Stem Cells*, 1:766.

12. Zoloth, "Immortal Cells, Moral Selves," 752.

13. Ibid., 753.

14. Lisa Sowle Cahill, book review of *The Human Embryonic Stem Cell Debate*, in *National Catholic Bioethics Quarterly*, 2:3:559-62 (Autumn 2002), 562.

15. Eric Juengst and Michael Fossel, "The Ethics of Embryonic Stem Cells—Now and Forever, Cells without End," *JAMA*, 284:24:3180-84 (December 27, 2000), 3181.

6. The Research Standards Framework

1. Donald W. Fink, "Human Embryonic Stem Cells: Regulatory Considerations," *Handbook of Stem Cells*, ed. Robert Lanza, 2 vols. (Amsterdam: Elsevier Academic Press, 2004), 1:775-786; and Stephen R. Bauer, "Stem Cell-Based Products in Medicine: FDA Regulatory Considerations," ibid., 2:805-814..

2. Christopher Thomas Scott, *Stem Cell Now* (New York: Pi Press, 2006),149.

3. Mary Warnock, *A Question of Life: The Warnock Report on Human Fertilization and Embryology* (Oxford: Blackwell, 1984).

4. *Guidelines for Human Embryonic Stem Cell Research*, National Research Council Institute of Medicine of the National Academies (Washington, D.C.: National Academies Press, 2005), http://newton.nap.edu/catalog/11278.html#toc.

5. California Institute for Regenerative Medicine, *Scientific and Medical Accountability Standards*, http://www.cirm.ca.gov/laws/pdfAdoptedRegs_100010.pdf.

6. Bioethics Advisory Committee of Singapore, *Ethical, Legal and Social Issues in Human Stem Cell*

Research, Reproductive and Therapeutic Cloning, report submitted to the Ministerial Committee for Life Sciences, June 2002. See the BAC Web site, http://www.bioethics-singapore.org/. Quotes following in text are from this source.

7. See: National Council of Churches of Singapore, *A Christian Response to the Life Sciences* (Singapore: Genesis, 2002).

8. CBC report on Canadian Institutes of Health Research guidelines on stem cell research: http://www.cbc.ca/news/story/2002/03/04/stemcells020304.html.

9. "The California Stem Cell Research and Cures Initiative" of 2004. The entire text of Proposition 71 is available on the web: http://www.cirm.ca.gov/prop71/pdf/prop71.pdf.

10. Suzanne Holland, "Beyond the Embryo: A Feminist Appraisal of the Embryonic Stem Cell Debate," *The Human Embryonic Stem Cell Debate: Science, Ethics, and Public Policy*, ed. Suzanne Holland, Karen Lebacqz, and Laurie Zoloth (Cambridge and London: MIT Press, 2001), 74.

11. For a longer treatment of the Hwang Woo Suk story, see: Michael Bellomo, *The Stem Cell Divide*, (New York: American Management Association, 2006), chapter 11.

12. Ronald M. Green, "Ethical Considerations," *Handbook of Stem Cells*, 1:762.

13. Holland, "Beyond the Embryo," 83.

7. Theological Reflections on Human Nature

1. Karl Barth, *Christ and Adam: Man and Humanity in Romans 5* (New York: Collier Books, 1956), 74-75.

2. Wolfhart Pannenberg, *Anthropology in Theological Perspective* (Louisville: Westminster John Knox Press, 1985), 497.

3. Wolfhart Pannenberg, *What Is Man?* (Minneapolis: Fortress Press, 1962), vii.

4. Ibid., 140.

5. Pannenberg, *Anthropology in Theological Perspective*, 527.

6. Catherine Mowry LaCugna, *God for Us: The Trinity and Christian Life* (San Francisco: Harper, 1991), 15.

7. Marjori Hewitt Suchocki, *The Fall to Violence: Original Sin in Relational Theology* (New York: Continuum, 1994), 73.

8. Ibid.

9. The Enlightenment criterion for the existence of inherent value is our capacity to reason. Rationality is the human quality that warrants dignity. Zygotes and blastocysts cannot reason. No one would require that the early embryo be responsible for meeting this criterion, to be sure. Yet embryo protectionists will argue that zygotes and blastocysts have the potential for reasoning in the future. Such an argument fails on two counts. First, such a vague potentiality is too far from being an actuality that could claim the moral warrant that dignity can claim. Second, the premise risks falsification because it places the warrant for dignity within the entity itself. By making dignity dependent upon a possessed quality, such as the capacity to reason or the potential to develop the capacity to reason, what goes unnoticed is the role that relationship plays in establishing dignity. And, theologically, it fails to notice the role that grace plays.

10. See: Ted Peters, *For the Love of Children: Genetic Technology and the Future of the Family* (Louisville, Ky.: Westminster John Knox Press, 1996), 52-54; and Ted Peters, "Love and Dignity: Against Children Becoming Commodities," *Genetic Testing*

and Screening, ed. Roger A. Willer (Minneapolis: Kirk House, 1998), 116-29; and "Embryonic Stem Cells and the Theology of Dignity," *The Human Embryonic Stem Cell Debate: Science, Ethics, and Public Policy*, ed. Suzanne Holland, Karen Lebacqz, and Laurie Zoloth (Cambridge and London: MIT Press, 2001), 127-40.

11. Karen Lebacqz, "Justice," *Christian Ethics*, ed. Bernard Hoose (Herndon, Va: Cassell, 1998).

12. Anne Foerst, *God in the Machine: What Robots Teach Us about Humanity and God* (New York: Dutton, 2004), 185.

13. Renee Mirkes, "NBAC and Embryo Ethics," *National Catholic Bioethics Quarterly* 1:2 (Summer 2001), 185.

14. David Bjerklie, Alice Park, and Dan Cray, "Inside the Womb," *Time* 160:20:68-78 (November 11, 2002), 70.

8. Can Theological Ethicists Help Anybody?

1. Ann A. Kiessling and Scott Anderson, *Human Embryonic Stem Cells* (Boston: Jones and Bartlett Publishers, 2003), 197.

2. Ronald Reagan Jr., quoted in Michael Bellomo, *The Stem Cell Divide*, (New York: American Management Association, 2006), 98.

3. Margaret A. Farley, "Stem Cell Research: Religious Considerations," *Handbook of Stem Cells*, ed. Robert Lanza, 2 vols. (Amsterdam: Elsevier Academic Press, 2004), 1:771.

4. Ronald M. Green, "Ethical Considerations," in ibid., 1:763.